ON BEING A BROAD CHURCH

Five Lectures

J. W. Rogerson

BEAUCHIEF
ABBEY·PRESS

Published by Beauchief Abbey Press.
Copyright © J W Rogerson, 2013
ISBN 978-0-9576841-2-6

CONTENTS

Introduction   v

Lectures:

1. Broad Church: Nineteenth Century Background   1
2. Broad Church: Scripture   17
3. Broad Church: Reason   32
4. Broad Church: Tradition   47
5. Broad Church Today   63

Bibliography   77
Index of Persons and Subjects   80
About the Author   82

INTRODUCTION

The term 'Broad Church' is generally thought to have appeared in print for the first time in an article by A. P. Stanley in the July 1850 issue of the *Edinburgh Review*, although the term appears to have been in use orally before that date.[1] In the course of time it came to denote a group of nineteenth century Anglicans, chief among whom were F. D. Maurice, Charles Kingsley and F. W. Robertson, for all that Maurice, certainly, vigorously denied that he belonged to any such 'party' in the Church of England. One of their principal sources of inspiration was the poet and literary scholar S. T. Coleridge. Their work has been seen to represent an outstanding achievement within the Church of England.

The aim of the 2013 Beauchief Abbey Lent Lectures was to introduce the audience to some of the main ideas of the broad churchmen, and to explore whether these ideas could inform today's church. The first lecture gives a historical introduction to the broad church. There then follow lectures on Scripture, Reason and Tradition, the three supposed foundation stones of Anglicanism. The final lecture suggests how a broad church today must be biblical, evangelical and catholic.

---

[1] See N. M. Distad, *Guessing at Truth. The Life of Julius Charles Hare*, Shepherdstown: The Patmos Press, 1979, pp. 157-160 for a discussion of the origin and application of the term.

I am grateful to the Beauchief Abbey congregation for inviting me to give the 2013 lectures, and I wish to thank all those who came out on some very raw winter evenings to hear the lectures and to discuss them with me afterwards. The congregation arranged for the lectures to be filmed, and they can be viewed on line via the Beauchief Abbey web site. This published version is part of the educational programme of the Abbey congregation, and it is to be hoped that readers will be able to engage with them more deeply with the leisure afforded by the printed text.

J. W. Rogerson

August 2013

LECTURE 1

Broad Church: Nineteenth Century Background

'What kind of church is it?' This is a question we might well ask a friend or acquaintance who has moved to a new town, and has started attending a local Anglican church. 'What kind of church is it?' The answer may be that it is Anglo-Catholic, or Evangelical, or Charismatic, or Liberal; and sometimes there are combinations of these labels, such as Liberal Catholic, or modifications such as 'mildly Charismatic'. Yet even these labels do not do justice to the variety of churches that can be found today under the umbrella of 'Anglicanism'. There are, at what we might unfairly call the extremes, hard-line evangelical and Anglo-Catholic churches, united in opposition, for different reasons, to ordained women's ministry, among other things. In between these extremes there are many shades of churchmanship. Over the years I have met many what I call 'faded evangelicals'. These are churches that maintain the externals of evangelicalism, such as insistence on the need for individuals to make a personal commitment to Jesus Christ as Lord and Saviour, and patterns of worship and ministry directed to that end. However if they are pressed to say whether they believe that anyone who does not make a personal commitment to Christ in this life will be punished eternally in hell, along with adherents of non-Christian religious faiths, they can become rather vague. Yet if they do not believe in hell and punishment, from what does Jesus save those who make a personal commitment? I well remember from my National Service days a Plymouth Brother who constantly reminded the Christian Fellowship to which we belonged that each minute thousands of souls were passing into eternal damnation, and that this thought should galvanise us into evangelistic activity. I sometimes get the impression that 'faded evangelical' churches lack urgency in what they do because they do not have any clear rationale for their evangelicalism.

Just as I have met 'faded evangelicals' I have met 'woolly sacramentalists'. These are often people who have moved from evangelicalism towards Anglo-Catholicism and embraced something like the theology of the liturgical movement of the 1950s and 1960s. The Eucharist is central to what they do, with the bread and wine representing the common things of life which God blesses and returns to the communicants. The mission of such churches seems to be to maintain a

Eucharistic ministry and to encourage parishioners to enjoy its benefits.

These sketches are no doubt caricatures, and almost certainly are not fair to the dedicated, prayerful work done in these churches. I apologise to anyone who thinks that I am criticising them personally. I am not. I am merely giving my impressions, which may of course be mistaken, of encounters with many types of churches over many years.

Whether or not my sketches are fair or accurate, I am convinced of one thing. I have never experienced in Britain anything like a German Lutheran church. There is, of course, the risk that I have become starry-eyed about a church of which I have little experience; but I can claim the following experience. I have on three occasions taken charge of a Lutheran congregation in Germany for a few weeks in the summer, and have taken baptisms, weddings and funerals in addition to Sunday services and other pastoral work. Perhaps more importantly I have twice led intensive courses for German theological students at residential summer academies, both lasting a fortnight. My impressions from these experiences, as well as attendance at many German Lutheran services, are as follows.

The most profound sermons that I have ever heard have been preached in German Lutheran services. (There have been many indifferent ones, of course!) I cannot think that such sermons would or could have been preached in an Anglican church. Secondly, the quality of students training for ordination in Germany is much, much higher than in England. I base this judgement upon having taught many ordinands during 15 years in Durham as well as acting as an External Examiner in a number of Anglican theological colleges for many years. The students I taught at the German summer academies were of much higher quality. It can be objected, of course, that I am concentrating on intellectual ability, and that because a person is clever, he or she will not necessarily be a good minister or priest. That is certainly true; but what impressed me about the German theological students was their profound understanding of what Christianity was about, compared with the frequent 'woolliness' of their English counterparts. My third impression is that theology and the church are taken far more seriously in Germany than in England in the public sphere. In England it is generally held that religion is a private, individual matter, and that the church is merely one of a number of 'faith groups' that operate for the benefit of their members. The churches in Germany, without being 'established' in the English sense, are taken much more seriously in the public sphere.

Where is this leading to? I have often asked myself why we cannot have in England something that resembles the German Lutheran churches – churches that are liberal and at the same time positive; churches that know what they *do* believe rather than knowing what they do *not* believe; churches that are able to attract into their ministry young people from the top 5% of academic ability; churches that are taken seriously in civic and national life. The answer to this question is that there is a tradition within Anglicanism that could fit this bill, the Broad

Church tradition of the nineteenth century. The purpose of these Abbey Lent Lectures will be to consider this tradition anew, and see what it might look like in the twenty-first century.

Before going into details, it is worth comparing the situation facing the Church of England in the middle of the nineteenth century with the situation facing it today. In the mid-nineteenth century the Church of England was deeply divided not, as today, over gender and ministry matters, but over Baptism, an issue that affected how one understood the nature of the church and its task. The mid-nineteenth century was a time of change and upheaval. The industrial revolution was transforming the country, as people moved from the country-side to the towns, to find employment that made them live in appalling slums, and which required their children to work for twelve hours a day, six days a week in mills and factories. Parliamentary reform was attacking the privileged position enjoyed by the church, while the Church Census of March 1851 revealed that in some parts of the country only a third of the population attended Sunday services, and that more worshippers went to Methodist services than to Anglican services. In Sheffield, for example, out of a population of 135,310, 43,421 had attended Sunday worship and this figure included those who had attended twice, as well as Sunday school children[2]. Anglican attendances had totalled 14,881, while the figure for Wesleyan, Primitive and New Connexion

---

[2] E. R. Wickham, *Church and People in an Industrial City*, London: Lutterworth Press, 1957, pp.108-9.

Methodists was 15,271. Just as today the presence of non-Christian religious communities in Britain has led to pressure for the Christian churches to be sidelined as merely one instance of many 'faith communities', so it was argued in the mid-nineteenth century that the Church of England no longer represented the majority of Christians in the land. (Thirty years later, in 1881, the situation had changed somewhat, with Anglican attendances in Sheffield easily outnumbering Methodist ones, although still amounting to only 40 per cent of total Sunday attendance.[3])

I shall focus in the present lecture on the response of four Anglicans to this situation: Julius Hare (1795-1855), Frederick Denison Maurice (1805-1872), Charles Kingsley (1819-1875) and Frederick William Robertson (1816-1853). Hare, Maurice and Kingsley were very close to each other. Hare had been Maurice's tutor at university, and Kingsley regarded Maurice as his great mentor. All three had connections to German thought directly or indirectly, and were friendly with Baron C. C. J. Bunsen, who was a Prussian diplomat in Britain, and himself a distinguished Old Testament scholar.[4] They were also deeply influenced by Samuel Taylor Coleridge, who had studied in Germany, had absorbed German idealist philosophy, and written theological works of great profundity.[5] Robertson did not strictly belong to this group, but in his short

---

[3] Wickham, *Church and People*, p.148

[4] See J.W. Rogerson, *Old Testament Criticism in the Nineteenth Century: England and Germany*, London: SPCK, 1984, pp.121-9.

[5] See the study of Coleridge in B. Willey, *Nineteenth-Century Studies. Coleridge to Matthew Arnold*, Harmondsworth: Penguin Books, 1964, pp. 9-58.

life, his sermons preached in Brighton made a deep impression on anyone who was looking for a fresh understanding of the Christian gospel in the mid-nineteenth century. His views were close to those of the others. The issue of Baptism shows how the 'broad church' group made a distinctive contribution to the theology and practice of the day.

The issue of Baptism, which divided the Church of England so sharply, and which was so important in the mid-nineteenth century, was brought to a head by the so called Gorham controversy. Article XXVII of the 39 Articles of Religion states that

> Baptism ... is a sign of Regeneration or new Birth

but what did this mean? High Churchmen took regeneration to mean that the original sin of a baptised infant was washed away and that the infant was given a new nature. Regeneration was equivalent to conversion. This view has been summed up as follows: 'Through baptism man receives a new nature, and thus a moral change takes place'[6] Such a view was quite unacceptable to the Evangelicals, for whom conversion, that is, a conscious decision to accept Jesus Christ as Saviour, was the only method of entry into the Church. Baptism gave a *claim* on the part of the baptised infant to be a recipient of the forgiveness and salvation offered in Jesus Christ. It did not alter the *nature* of a baptised child; it altered the child's *status* as a potential recipient of a new nature.[7]

---

[6] P.J.Jagger, *Clouded Witness. Initiation in the Church of England in The Mid-Victorian Period, 1850-1875*, Pennsylvania: Pickwick Publications, 1982, p.16.
[7] See Jagger, *Clouded Witness*, pp.16-24.

These two views of baptism radically affected how the High Church and Evangelical parties understood the task of the Church. For High Churchmen, the task was to build upon what infants had received in baptism. For Evangelicals the task was to bring the unconverted baptised infant to a personal decision for Christ. I shall not say much about the Gorham controversy, which arose when Bishop Philpotts of Exeter, a High Churchman, refused to institute the Revd. G. C. Gorham, an Evangelical, to a living in his diocese, on the ground that Gorham held a view of regeneration contrary to the teaching of the Church of England. For Gorham, baptism conferred a new nature only if it was worthily received.[8] Gorham appealed, and it was eventually decided by the Judicial Committee of the Privy Council that his views were not contrary to the declared doctrine of the Church of England.

However, there was a third way of approaching the matter, and this was strongly expressed by F. W. Robertson in two sermons preached in March 1850, at the time of the Gorham judgement. His objection to the Roman Catholic view, a view that he said was embraced in various ways by Anglican High Churchmen, was that if a rite or ceremony (i.e. Baptism) was duly and properly performed, original sin was removed, there was a change of nature, and a new character was imparted, whether or not the recipient was aware of this or responded to it.[9] The Calvinist view made being a child of God dependent

---

[8] F.W. Cornish, *The English Church in the Nineteenth Century*, Part I, London: Macmillan & Co, 1910, pp. 319-336.
[9] F.W. Robertson, *Sermons Preached at Brighton*, Second Series, London: Kegan Paul, Trench,1889, p.46

upon having particular religious experiences. According to Robertson, Rome and Calvinism were both wrong because they tried to *create a fact*: Rome by baptising and Calvinism by insisting on certain religious experiences. However, the *fact* was that all children, when they are born, are children of God. Baptism cannot create this fact, it can only affirm it. Conversion cannot create this fact, it can only acknowledge it. As Robertson said:

> Baptism does not *create* a child of God. It authoritatively declares him so. It does not make the fact: it only reveals it.[10]

He went on to criticise the view that a person is *not* a child of God until baptism has been administered, or until a person been converted. Similar views were held by Maurice and Kingsley[11] and Kingsley drew profound implications for the social problems of his day.

> How dare you, in the face of that Baptismal sign... keep God's children exposed to filth, brutality and temptation, which fester in your courts and alleys, making cleanliness impossible - drunkenness all but excusable – prostitution all but natural – self-respect and decency unknown?[12]

Theologically, the view of Robertson, Maurice and Kingsley was a claim that the Christian church had a universal function. It was there not simply to look after its own interests and members, but to carry out the implications of Genesis 1 that the universe was created by God and that human kind was

---

[10] Robertson: *Sermons*, p.56.

[11] See Jagger, *Clouded Witness* p.28-39.

[12] Quoted in Jagger, *Clouded Witness* p.33

created in God's image. Baptism was a public declaration of this fact. 'Baptism', declared Robertson, 'is a visible witness to the world of that which the world is for ever forgetting. A common Humanity united in God.'[13]

It is instructive to pause for a moment to compare this vision with baptismal practice in the Church of England today. Baptism seems to have been reduced to a rite of entry into the church, with not a few parishes refusing it to families that do not regularly attend worship, and offering instead a service of thanksgiving for the birth of the child. Here at the Abbey, it is certainly my view that we are acting in the spirit of Robertson and the others, and are declaring publicly that the children brought for baptism are the children of God, with all that that implies for the nature of society and the church's task to declare and express the lordship of God over every area of human life.

At the beginning of Robertson's second sermon on baptism there is an important observation that leads on to the next part of this lecture. Robertson wrote that the truth, for him, did not lie 'in a middle course between the two extremes (of Romish and modern Calvinistic views) but in a truth deeper than either of them'.[14] This could be taken as a definition of what has come to be called the 'broad church', a label thoroughly disliked by Maurice and Kingsley. They were not trying to find a middle way, but a deeper way. I shall be saying a lot

---

[13] Robertson, *Sermons*, p.55
[14] Robertson, *Sermons*, p.60.

about this deeper way in the course of these lectures, but I shall give a hint about its origin and nature now.

In an essay written by F. D. Maurice about his former mentor and tutor, Julius Hare, Maurice mentioned that Hare's aunt had once wished that he would burn all his German books. She was expressing the view, common in England around 1820, that the critical thought that was being applied in Germany to the Bible, Christian tradition and theology was destroying Christianity and ruining the church.[15] Hare wrote to her in January 1820 as follows:

> As for my German books, I hope, from my heart that the day will never arrive when I shall be induced to burn them... I shall never be able to repay an hundredth part of the obligations I am under to them... for to them I owe the best of all my knowledge, and if they have not purified my heart, the fault is my own. Above all, to them I owe my ability to believe in Christianity, with a much more implicit and intelligent faith than I otherwise should have been able to have done.[16]

Hare was expressing what others were finding then, and have found since, that the German Lutheran tradition offered such a profound understanding of the nature of Christianity that it could welcome critical academic thought and enable people to be both critical and believing. A hint of the part played by Coleridge in making this possible for English churchmen came in the following passage in Maurice's essay. He spoke of those

---

[15] See further my *Old Testament Criticism*, pp.166-170.
[16] J. C. Hare, *Charges to the Clergy of the Archdeaconry of Lewes*, Cambridge: (edited and with an introduction by F. D. Maurice), Macmillan & Co, 1856, p.xiii.

who had come to believe that 'man is not an animal carrying about a soul, but a spiritual being with an animal nature, who, when he has sunk lowest into that nature, has still thoughts and recollections of a home to which he belongs, and from which he has wandered'.[17] Such people asked 'where is that home... how can we ever come to it?' Coleridge had taught that even if science had become Omniscience, it could not interpret that cry for a Living God. Coleridge had taught that people should not give up their search, but should follow it tirelessly until it brought them to their Father's house.

For me this is a profound description of what is often called, disparagingly, 'folk religion' and explains why this Abbey is filled to overflowing on Christmas Eve, and why people who do not normally come to church want to bring their babies to be baptised. The challenge, especially to a Broad Church, is to help people find an answer to the question 'where is that home from which we seem to have wandered... how can we ever come to it?'

- - - - -

F. D. Maurice's contribution to the deep thinking that characterised his circle was based on his understanding of Genesis 1. God had created the universe, and humankind in his own image. It followed that all human life was hallowed, and that God intended that there should be a spiritual society or kingdom that enabled God's children to live together in love and harmony under his lordship. The Bible bore witness

---

[17] Hare, *Charges*, p.xxi.

to this spiritual kingdom in the story of the Israelite people and in the teaching of Jesus about the Kingdom of God. This spiritual kingdom was not identical with the church or the nation state, although both embodied aspects of it. It was the task of the church to bear witness to the existence of this spiritual kingdom, and to endeavour to see that it was made visible in the daily lives of ordinary people.

In a sermon on priesthood preached in May 1851, Maurice criticised clergy who thought of themselves as belonging to a class that was jealous of its own privileges, power and prestige. No! We clergy...

> are sent into the world... to bear witness for the consecration and the holiness of God's entire family. We become guilty.... when by our words or acts we lead you to think that you have not received this consecration, that you are not set apart to God; that you and your children and your occupations are not holy in His sight.[18]

However, the task of proclaiming that all human enterprise was sacred to God also entailed judgement. It was also the duty of the priest to proclaim that all 'disorders and anomalies' were contrary to God's will and that 'statesmen as well as churchmen, instead of tolerating and excusing them, ought to be labouring day and night for the removal of them'.[19]

Given these views, it is no surprise that Maurice had wide-ranging social concerns. Together with Kingsley and J.M.

---

[18] F. D. Maurice, *The Patriarchs and Lawgivers of the Old Testament*, London: Macmillan & Co, 1892
[19] Maurice, *Patriarchs and Lawgivers*, pp.218-9.

Ludlow, he met on the evening of 10 April 1848 following the great Chartist demonstration on Kennington Common, to discuss action, and two days later, joined by J. C. Hare and Alexander J. Scott, decided to launch a newspaper entitled 'Politics for the people'. This was the beginning of the Christian Socialist movement of 1848, and in a Tract on Christian Socialism Maurice declared that it was necessary to get rid of the idea 'that Christ is the Head of a set of religious men, the Head of a sect of Christians' and to believe 'that He is actually the Son of God and the Son of Man'.[20] Maurice and his circle helped to organise Higher Education for Women, and they became involved in Trades Associations and industrial disputes. Kingsley's novels *Alton Locke* and *The Water Babies* sought to bring a Christian perspective to the social problems of his day.

No account of the theology of the 'broad church' circle can be complete unless we deal with that most important theological question of all: how did the ministry and the death of Jesus bridge the gulf between God and humanity, a gulf created by the evil and wickedness of the human race? Robertson addressed this in a sermon preached in June 1850 entitled The Sacrifice of Christ. He took as his text 2 Corinthians 5.14-15.

> For the love of Christ, constraineth us; because we thus judge, that if one died for all, then were all dead; and that he died for all that they which live should not henceforth live unto themselves, but unto him which died for them, and rose again'.

---

[20] Quoted in C. E. Raven, *Christian Socialism 1848-1854*, London: Frank Cass & Co., 1968, p.90

Robertson made the following points:

> There was scarcely a form of evil with which Christ did not come into contact, and by which he did not suffer. He was the victim of false friendship and ingratitude, the victim of bad government and injustice. He fell a sacrifice to the vices of all classes, - to the selfishness of the rich and the fickleness of the poor: - intolerance, formalism, suspicion, hatred of goodness, were the foes which crushed him.[21]

And he did this on behalf of all.

> If you have been a false friend, a sceptic, cowardly disciple, a formalist, selfish, an opposer of goodness, an oppressor, whatever evil you have done... you are one of that mighty rabble which cry 'Crucify Him!'.

Yet Christ is also the example of perfect humanity. He is God's idea of man completed. He offers to God the sacrifice that only he can offer, that of perfect suffering love on behalf of others, and God, in accepting that sacrifice accepts sinful humanity for Christ's sake. We cannot approach God on our own behalf. We can only do so by recognizing that Christ has done for us what we could not do for ourselves; and that this is all the Father's work. The following verse from a well-known hymn sums up the position concisely:

> Look Father, look on his anointed face,
> And only look on us as found in him;
> Look not on our misusings of Thy grace,
> Our prayer so languid and our faith so dim:
> For lo, between our sins and their reward
> We set the Passion of Thy Son our Lord.

---

[21] Robertson, *Sermons*, p. 96

In the remaining lectures I shall ask how we can formulate a 'broad church' theology for today. Not one that tries to find a middle way, but one that tries to find a deeper way.

LECTURE 2

Broad Church: Scripture

In 1862, F.D. Maurice read the first volume of J.W. Colenso's book *The Pentateuch and Book of Joshua Critically Examined*, which had just been published.[22] Maurice was devastated by what he read. The two men were, in fact, close friends. Colenso had much admired Maurice's book *The Kingdom of Christ*, and Maurice had officiated at Colenso's wedding in 1846. He much admired Colenso's work as a missionary bishop to the Zulu in the British colony of Natal in South Africa. Colenso had not only converted many Zulu to Christianity. He had written a dictionary and grammar of Zulu and had translated the Bible into Zulu. He had begun to instruct his converts to teach the Christian faith to their fellow tribesmen, and he was undoubtedly one of the greatest

---

[22] J. W. Colenso, *The Pentateuch and Book of Joshua Critically Examined*, London: Longman, Green, Longman, Roberts & Green, 1862.

missionary bishops of his time. Why, then, was Maurice so distressed when he read Colenso's book?

Colenso had attacked the way in which the Bible described the Israelite crossing of the Red Sea, and the subsequent Wilderness Wanderings. The Book of Exodus (Exodus 12.37) says that 600,000 male Israelites left Egypt at the time of the Exodus. However, if there were 600,000 men the total population must have been around two million. Yet, according to the Bible, only seventy Israelites had gone down into Egypt four generations previously. How had they become so numerous in so short a time? The two million people together with their sheep and cattle and carts would have taken up an enormous amount of space, and as they journeyed towards the Red Sea the column would have been some twenty-two miles long, so that the last of the party could not have started the crossing until the front had advanced twenty-two miles, something that would have taken at least two days.[23] There were many other difficulties attending the account in the Bible. For example, there were said to be only three priests at the time. This being so, they would have had to slaughter the lambs at the time of the Passover at the rate of 1000 a minute, and when they presented the offerings required for new-born children they would have needed to work for nearly 42 hours a day![24] Colenso was not the first person to discover these difficulties with the text as taken literally. They had been long recognised, and orthodox scholars had found ways of defending the text.

---

[23] Colenso, *Pentateuch*, pp. 63-4.
[24] See further J.W. Rogerson, *Old Testament Criticism in the Nineteenth Century*, pp. 222-3.

But Colenso was not prepared to accept the unconvincing and special pleading which was required for the defence of the biblical text, and he felt obliged to say that the text could not be true at the level of credible history. Again, he was not the first person to say this; but what scandalised the English establishment of his day was the fact that Colenso was an Anglican bishop, for whom such ideas were unforgivable.

Why did Colenso do this? He tells us in his own words:

> While translating the story of the Flood, I have had a simple-minded, but intelligent, native, - one with the of the docility of a child, but the reasoning powers of a mature age, - look up, and ask, 'Is all that true? Do you really believe that all this happened thus, - that all the beasts, and birds, and creeping things, upon the earth, large and small, from hot countries and cold, came thus by pairs, and entered into the ark with Noah? And did Noah gather food for them *all*, for the beasts and birds of prey, as well as the rest? My heart answered in the words of the Prophet, 'Shall a man speak lies in the Name of the LORD?' Zech. xiii.3. I dared not do so. My own knowledge of some branches of science, of Geology in particular, had been much increased since I left England; and I now knew for certain, on geological grounds, a fact, of which I had only had misgivings before, viz. that a *Universal* deluge, such as the Bible manifestly speaks of, could not possibly have taken place in the way described in the Book of Genesis, not to mention other difficulties which the story contains...I felt that I dared not, as a servant of the God of Truth, urge my brother man to believe that, which I did not myself believe, which I knew to be untrue, as a matter-of-fact, historical, narrative. I gave him, however, such a reply as satisfied him for the time...but I was thus driven, against my will at first, I may truly say, to search more deeply into these questions.[25]

---

[25] Colenso, *Pentateuch*, pp. vii-viii.

In the first volume of his investigations, Colenso did not deal with the Flood and Noah's ark, the narrative that had sparked off his study of biblical criticism. This came in the second part of volume four several years later, and Colenso was devastating in his exposure of the implications of the story as taken literally. He pictured how the ark was inhabited, with snails and insects as well as animals, not forgetting insects that did not normally go in pairs, such as bees. He described the life of Noah and his family keeping animals such as lions well away from their normal prey, such as sheep, but needing additional animals in order to feed the carnivores. He pictured Noah and his family renewing the litter of the animals and disposing of their excrement. He wondered how, after the ark had grounded on Mount Ararat, the flightless Dodo had got to the island of Mauritius, or the kangaroo had reached Australia.

For Maurice, all this was devastating. For him, the Old Testament was a true account of God's dealings with the Israelite people, an account that revealed what God was like, and how he had established his government in the world through his dealings with the Israelite people. He felt that Colenso was attacking this belief, and in the process undermining all that he, Maurice, stood for. Kingsley was similarly distressed by Colenso's views, and published a book of sermons entitled *The Gospel of the Pentateuch*, and in the preface, without naming Colenso, he expressed his deep dissatisfaction.[26]

---

[26] C. Kingsley, *The Gospel of the Pentateuch. A Set of Parish Sermons*, London: Parker, Son, and Bourn, 1863.

One hundred and fifty years later we know that Colenso was right and that Maurice and Kingsley were wrong in their opposition to him. By 1862, Hare and Robertson were both dead, so we do not know how they would have reacted. The question for a modern broad church is how we can accept the findings of biblical criticism while still maintaining the position of a man such as Maurice who drew such important consequences from the Bible for Christian faith and practice. The same question arises with regard to the New Testament. The critical study of the four gospels has led some people to suggest that the interpretation of Jesus by the church as the Son of God is incorrect, and that from the critical study of the gospels, we can discover the true historical Jesus, rather than the Christ of faith which the church has made him into. There have been several recent books by distinguished scholars that have tried to do precisely this, while at the level of what we might call the lunatic fringe, there have been books suggesting that Jesus married Mary Magdalene, had a family, and carried on living after the crucifixion. For the remainder of this lecture I shall deal first of all with the Old Testament and how critical scholarship affects our understanding of it, before passing to a consideration of the gospels as a witness to the life and ministry of Jesus.

Since 1862, archaeological discoveries have transformed our knowledge of the ancient world in which the Old Testament was written. Texts from ancient Assyria and Babylon have shown us that the story of the Flood in the Old Testament was commonly known in the ancient world. We now know much about the history of those great nations, Egypt, Babylon and

Assyria, that played such an important part in the history of Israel, and about which we knew previously only from the Old Testament and some classical sources. We also know that many of the laws in the Book of Exodus can be paralleled from the laws from ancient Babylonia and Assyria, and this, of course, was the subject of the Beauchief Abbey lectures last year. Many of the great sites in ancient Israel have been excavated, such as Megiddo, Lachish, Samaria, and Hazor. Excavations in Jerusalem have been limited by the fact of its continued occupation, but such work as has been done has greatly contributed to our knowledge of its history. Archaeologists do not always agree, however! According to one school of thought, archaeology reveals that Jerusalem was not really occupied much before the time of David, and that the biblical account of the empire of David and Solomon has been somewhat exaggerated. I have no time this evening to go into the disputes between the so-called minimalists and the so-called maximalists.[27] My own view of the history of Israel is that a distinctive people, united by common religious beliefs, began to emerge sometime in the 10th to 9th centuries BC. A large part was played in this by prophetic groups who believed in a God called Yahweh who demanded social justice and that rulers should rule fairly and justly. Not everyone agreed, of course, and many of the people had recourse to popular beliefs and superstitions. In the early part of the 9th century an able ruler named Omri established a powerful

---

[27] See my essay 'Israel to the End of the Persian Period: History, Social, Political and Economic Background' in J. W. Rogerson, Judith M. Lieu, (eds.), *The Oxford Handbook of Biblical Studies*, Oxford: Oxford University Press, 2006, pp. 268-284.

kingdom in the north of Israel which dominated the region for fifty or so years. Omri and his descendants were bitterly opposed by the prophetic groups, who preserved some of the ancient traditions of the people. During this time, there was a smaller, and weaker Israelite kingdom to the south named Judah, one of whose founding kings had been named David. Following the destruction of the northern kingdom in the year 721 the kingdom of Judah took over the role of Israel and scribal and prophetic groups began to write down the ancient traditions of the two peoples. Judah was destroyed by the Babylonians in 597 and 587 and the king and the notable people of Judah were deported to Babylon. This tragedy led to deeper reflection on the part of the prophetic and priestly groups. It gave great stimulus to the writing down of the ancient traditions, including the prophetic books, the stories about the founding fathers, the Exodus from Egypt, and the giving of the laws to Moses. What we call today the Old Testament began to take shape, and it reached something like its present and final form two hundred years before the birth of Jesus.

It has long been accepted that the Bible is not an up-to-date handbook on matters of science, astronomy, geography, and technology. The great reformer, Calvin, for example, commenting on Genesis 1 which talks about the two great lights, i.e., the sun and the moon, and who was aware that the telescope had made it apparent that there were much bigger heavenly bodies in the universe than the moon, advised his readers that the biblical account described the universe only as it could be observed with the naked eye. 'He who would learn astronomy', wrote Calvin, 'let him go elsewhere'.[28] It is a pity that those, today, who want to take Genesis literally, do not study the history of biblical interpretation. If they did, they would discover that there have been many different ways of interpreting Genesis 1, and certainly by scholars whose Christian commitment to the Bible could in no way be doubted. However, even some critical scholars who have been happy to accept that the Bible is not an accurate handbook on matters of geography, astronomy and physics, have been reluctant to accept that the same applies to its historical records. There have been a number of rear-guard actions designed to protect the historical accuracy of the Old Testament. However, today, critical scholarship speaks more in terms of cultural memory than history, and this is an important way of interpreting the Old Testament historical narratives correctly.

The easiest way to understand cultural memory is to think in terms of a water filter. Here in Sheffield, with our splendid Yorkshire water, we do not need water filters, but I once visited a friend in Lincolnshire who filtered all his water before using it. You put the water into the top of the container, and as it trickles down to the bottom, it passes through various layers of filters which remove the impurities. Cultural memory is similar in the following way. Memories are passed down from generation to generation, and as they descend, they may be telescoped, while bad memories may be forgotten and good memories are retained. Part of the remembering process may

---

[28] J. Calvin, *Genesis*, Edinburgh: Banner of Truth Trust, 1965 (orig. 1578) p.79

be connected with religious celebrations and liturgical recitations, and this is certainly true of the story of the Exodus and the Wilderness Wanderings, which are still commemorated yearly at Passover time by Jewish Communities. What we have in the narratives of the Old Testament are filtered cultural memories, and the question arises how we are to interpret them. In our discussion following the lecture last week I mentioned the important distinction between UNDERSTANDING and REASON as formulated by Coleridge. I said that UNDERSTANDING was concerned with facts, while REASON was concerned with meaning. If we take these concepts to the story of the Exodus, we have to say that from the standpoint of UNDERSTANDING, that is, as concerning facts, we can find many faults with the story and its arithmetic. If we ask the question 'what does this story mean?' we have to say that it contains the experience of many generations of Israelites of their encounter with God and their belief that God was guiding the affairs of their nation both for salvation and for judgement. In the ethical teaching of the Old Testament, the Exodus story played an important role, as I showed in my lectures last year. The Israelites were constantly reminded that they were once slaves in the land of Egypt and that God redeemed them from slavery, and therefore it was necessary for them to deal graciously with each other in order to reflect how God had been gracious to them. If we understand the narrative parts of the Old Testament as cultural memory and approach to them via REASON, that is, asking what they mean, we get a different answer compared with treating them as matter-of-fact history to be read from the standpoint of UNDERSTANDING.

I have on more than one occasion at the Abbey reminded you that it is remarkable that we have an Old Testament at all. Culturally, Israel and Judah were backward and undeveloped compared with the great civilisations of Egypt, Babylon, and Assyria. If you go to the Near Eastern Museum in Berlin, you can see a reconstruction of the Processional Way of the goddess Ishtar in Babylon, using the original wonderful enamelled bricks with a blue surface adorned by mythical figures in yellow and gold. This Processional Way dates from the time when the Israelites were in exile in Babylon and it must have been a source of great amazement to them. Yet it was not Egypt, Babylon, or Assyria that gave great ideas to the ancient world. These kingdoms disappeared, only to be rediscovered in the 19th century by the spades of the archaeologists. These kingdoms did not, like Israel and Judah, bequeath to the world what we call ethical monotheism, that is, belief in one God who demanded justice from and for all peoples. The preservation of the religious records, prophetic books, psalms and wisdom texts from ancient Israel over a period of three-and-a-half thousand years is to me adequate proof that God was involved with that people and with the scriptures that they gave to the world. A modern broad church use of the Old Testament must welcome every aspect of biblical criticism, yet understand what is the exact nature of the material that the Old Testament contains, and how it should be interpreted. The value of the Old Testament is that it is the witness of ordinary people facing many of the kinds of problems that we face today, and doing so with a deep awareness of the presence of God in their history and in their personal lives. This is one reason why texts such as the psalms still have so much to say to us in situations of sickness, distress, and joy. To lose the Old Testament either through ignorance or through an unwillingness to read it with the help of biblical criticism, is to lose a vital witness to the involvement of God in the world which he has created.

I turn now to the New Testament and to the question whether the gospels truly represent that Jesus Christ in whom the church believes, or whether biblical criticism has shown that the church has from the beginning been mistaken about him. One writer has summarised the problem neatly as follows. 'Christianity stands or falls by the historic figure of Jesus, yet the Christian conception of Jesus can never be demonstrated as the only possible interpretation of the evidence'.[29] This is why attempts have been made to show that Jesus was some kind of social reformer, or a type of wandering philosopher, or simply a great teacher, but certainly not the Son of God. In approaching this problem I want to mention the work of a great Methodist New Testament scholar who for fifteen years was my colleague in Durham, and whose seminar on the New Testament I attended each week for those fifteen years. His name was C. K. Barrett, and he died in the August of 2011. He was, interestingly enough, given the names of Charles Kingsley out of respect by his parents for that great churchman whom we mentioned last week.

---

[29] N. Micklem, 'A Modern Approach to Christology' in G. K. A. Bell, A. Deissmann (eds.), *Mysterium Christi. Christological Studies by British and German Theologians*, London: Longmans, Green & Co., 1930, p. 151

In an essay in the *Cambridge History of the Bible* entitled 'The Interpretation of the Old Testament in the New', Barrett examined all the ways in which the Old Testament was being used and interpreted by Jewish groups at the time of the ministry of Jesus.[30] After an exhaustive examination Barrett concluded that the way in which the Old Testament was used in the New Testament was without parallel at that time, and he concluded that there was only one possible explanation. 'The gospel story as a whole differs so markedly from current interpretation of the Old Testament that it is impossible to believe that it originated simply in meditations on prophecy; it originated in the career of Jesus of Nazareth'.[31] If I may add my own observations here as an Old Testament specialist, and also one who has made an extensive study of Jewish traditions of the time of Jesus, the remarkable thing about the ministry of Jesus is that it is so unexpected. No one reading the Old Testament in the way that it was being read in the time of Jesus could possibly have seen Jesus as the Servant of God sent to suffer and to rise from the dead. This is why, as the gospel records show, his ministry produced so much misunderstanding. Not only was he misunderstood by the religious authorities of his day, he was misunderstood by his own disciples. When he began to teach them that he must be delivered to the gentiles and must suffer at their hands, even his closest disciples refused to believe this. The reason why, at the crucifixion, the disciples deserted him, was because they could not believe that what

---

[30] C. K. Barrett, 'The Interpretation of the Old Testament in the New', in P. R. Ackroyd, C. F. Evans (eds.), *The Cambridge History of the Bible. From the Beginnings to Jerome*, Cambridge: Cambridge University Press, 1970, pp. 377-411.
[31] Barrett, 'Interpretation', p. 405.

was happening was the will of God. It was only after his Resurrection that they began to remember what he had taught them about his ministry and death, and they could begin to see that it was in fulfilment of the scriptures, even though no one saw this at the time. This, together with a number of other considerations, leaves me in no doubt that the church did not from the beginning misunderstand Jesus, or that his real mission was not quite different from what the church thought. At the end of his book *Jesus and the Gospel Tradition* Barrett made the following comment on the fact that Jesus, wrongly, seems to have expected the world to end shortly after the conclusion of his ministry. Barrett wrote,

> by being mistaken in detail, Jesus was more effectively shown to be right in all that really mattered than he could have been by small-scale accuracy. At the same time, he was shown to be very man, subject to our infirmity. Perhaps this is why, not least when we study the gospels with the most stringent historical discipline, he speaks to us as the word of God, in our speech.[32]

Just as the narrative traditions in the Old Testament are cultural memory, so the gospels of the New Testament are cultural memory, having been filtered through the experiences of the first disciples following the great crisis of the death and resurrection of Jesus, and their conviction that he was indeed God's chosen Servant for the salvation of his people and for the whole world. Just as we need to treat the cultural memories of the Old Testament from the standpoint of UNDER-STANDING and REASON, so we have to treat the gospel records

---

[32] C. K. Barrett, *Jesus and the Gospel Tradition*, London: SPCK, 1967, p. 108.

from the point of view of UNDERSTANDING and REASON. When we do so, we discover, as Barrett says, that Jesus speaks to us as the word of God, in our speech.

I want to end where I began, with Colenso's work on the Pentateuch. It must be remembered that Colenso was not a negative biblical critic. He was a missionary bishop, driven by a deep desire to teach the people among whom he worked, of the love of God expressed in Jesus Christ. But he was driven to do what he did with biblical criticism because he believed himself to serve the God of truth. It is tragic that he was misunderstood not only by the establishment of his day, which hated him deeply, but by his friends Maurice and Kingsley. He has been misunderstood frequently since. There is a widespread belief today, including in many churches, that anyone who practises biblical criticism must by definition be a non-believer or a disturber of the Christian faith. I hope that I have shown in this lecture that this is not the case, and that we have nothing to fear from biblical criticism. Indeed, I will go further and say that without biblical criticism we cannot present Christianity as an intelligible, convincing, and practical faith in our generation; and I have often said in sermons here in the Abbey that no other great world religion has had its scriptures subjected to such searching academic criticism as has been the case for the Bible. Similarly, no founder of a great religion has had his life subjected to such searching academic criticism as has Jesus. This is something that should give us pride and confidence. Yet I want to let Colenso have the last word in this lecture. At the end of Part Six of his great work on the Pentateuch he wrote the following memorable words,

There is no infallible Book for our guidance, as there is no infallible Church or infallible Man. The father of spirits has not willed it thus, who knows best what is needed for the education of each individual soul, as well as that of the race. But he gives us light enough upon our path that we may do our work here faithfully and fear no evil. And the pure in heart will see God face to face in many a page of the Sacred Book - will recognise the Divine Revelation of all that is good and true throughout it - will hear God's voice, and feel his Living Word come home to the heart, and that it must be obeyed.[33]

---

[33] Colenso, *Pentateuch* Part 6, p. 626.

LECTURE 3

Broad Church: Reason

A few weeks ago, I preached a sermon in the Abbey in which I expressed my dislike of the hymn 'All things bright and beautiful'. This hymn, unfortunately, is sometimes chosen by groups that come to the Abbey for the baptism of their children, and we usually manage to cut it down to three verses and the chorus! Why do I dislike it? I do so, because I think it leads people, especially young people, to doubt rather than belief, and to agnosticism rather than certainty. I can illustrate this by adding two verses that you will not normally find in the hymn books:

The greenfly on the roses,
The black fly on the beans,
The little hairy caterpillars
Gobbling up the greens.

Or how about this rather more sinister verse?

The earthquake and tsunami,
The devastating flood,
These surely make us wonder
If God is really good.

To these new verses I can add an incident that I have never forgotten from my days in the Royal Air Force. There was a compulsory chaplain's hour, and the chaplain tried to prove the existence of God to the assembled airmen by using an approach similar to that in the hymn 'All things bright and beautiful'. He was describing the order and beauty of nature and how this pointed to the existence of God, until one of those present interrupted him with the question, 'what about lice, padre'? In vain did the chaplain try to explain the importance of lice in God's purposes and the great chain of life, and how that chain would be fatally compromised if there were no lice in the world. At the end of that hour the chaplain had done more to sow doubt in the minds of his listeners than any sort of faith or conviction. He had made the very simple mistake of supposing that God must be an object within our world of time and space whose existence there could be proved by logical or rational argument. It is a mistake that people make all the time, and it is at the heart of the present-day attack on Christian belief by the atheist constituency. Worse still, it was the centrepiece of an Anglican programme for Sunday School teaching in the 1960s entitled 'Alive in

God's World', in which the children taking part were shown the wonders of nature in the churchyard and surrounding gardens. I wonder if they saw many slugs, or birds being caught by cats, and I wonder how these things were explained to be parts of God's purposes! The trouble with this approach is that the world of nature is highly ambiguous and if it points to any kind of God it does not point unambiguously to a loving God, or, indeed, the God of the Bible. I wonder how many Sunday School children were introduced to agnosticism by this church scheme in the 1960s!

This approach overlooks the important distinction between REASON and UNDERSTANDING, which is the subject of today's lecture, but before I pass on to that I must make an important observation about the biblical belief that the world is created by God. The Old Testament writers did not live, as did Mrs. Alexander, the writer of the hymn 'All things bright and beautiful', in rural Ireland with its temperate climate, but in the harsh world of the so-called Fertile Crescent in the Middle East, where rainfall was uncertain, and crops vital for the sustenance of life could be devastated by blight, mildew and locusts, to name some of the perils listed in Amos 4. The Hebrew word for famine (ra'āv) occurs over one hundred times in the Old Testament, and a number of stories in the Old Testament have famine as their background. Abram and his family go down to Egypt from Canaan because of famine, in Genesis 12. The story of Joseph, which explains why the Hebrews were in Egypt before the Exodus, has as its background the seven fat years followed the seven lean years of famine, while the book of Ruth begins with the words 'In the days when the Judges judged, there was a famine in the land.' It is this famine that causes the family of Naomi to go from Bethlehem to Moab, the event that triggers off the plot of the Book of Ruth.

When the Israelites and their neighbours in Canaan and Babylon and Assyria looked at the world around them, it did not speak to them of a loving Creator God. For the non-Israelite nations, the supernatural powers that had created the world were in conflict with each other, with the human race suffering the 'collateral damage' of their disputes. Israel's belief in a single Creator God, as expressed so marvellously, for example, in Isaiah 40, did not come from observation of 'All things bright and beautiful' but from the involvement of God in the life of the nation for judgement and salvation; from spiritual insight, not from logical reasoning.

The distinction between UNDERSTANDING and REASON was at the centre of the thought of Samuel Taylor Coleridge. It was set out in his book 'Aids to Reflection' published in 1825.[34] By UNDERSTANDING, Coleridge meant that facility of the mind that dealt with observable, empirical things. By REASON he meant that facility of the mind that dealt with non material things, including spiritual and aesthetic experiences. Making this distinction enabled Coleridge to break free from the mechanical and materialist thinking with which he had grown up, and

---

[34] S. T. Coleridge, *Aids to Reflection in the Formation of a Manly Character on the Several Grounds of Prudence, Morality and Religion,* London: George Routledge & Sons (no date).
Aphorism CVI deals with Reason and Understanding.

which dominated much philosophical thought in Britain in the 18th century.[35] For this kind of thought God was very much a part of the visible universe, and governed by its laws. Coleridge made this distinction for several reasons. First, it was impossible for UNDERSTANDING to explain why writers such as Shakespeare and Milton were acknowledged to be so great. Second, UNDERSTANDING could not explain why poets such as Wordsworth could write poetry about nature and the human soul which could resonate so deeply with those who read or heard it. Thirdly, Coleridge had studied German idealist philosophy, especially the critical philosophy of Kant. In his first two critiques, Kant had made a distinction between pure reason and practical reason. The first dealt with our empirical knowledge, the second with our moral knowledge, and Kant had argued that to say that the world was created could only be done on the basis of our moral knowledge, not our empirical knowledge.[36]

Let me try to illustrate the difference as follows. Imagine that you were born into and grew up in a stately home. It had many rooms, and many things to be explored, such as libraries. However, you were never been allowed to go out of the house. Indeed, there were people in the house who told you that there was no outside, and that the whole of reality was what you saw inside the house. However, you sometimes looked through a window and thought that you saw things

---

[35] See, for example, Basil Willey, 'S. T. Coleridge (1772-1834)' in B. Willey, *The English Moralists*, London: Methuen, 1965, pp. 296-312.
[36] See F. Copleston, *A History of Philosophy*, volume VI: Wolff to Kant, London: Burns and Oates, 1964, pp. 286-307.

outside, such as trees and birds. When you told this to the others in the house they told you that you were mistaken. There was no outside, and what you thought you saw was a reflection of what was inside, or a product of your imagination.

This is what happens if you think that the whole of reality can be described in terms of UNDERSTANDING, that is, in terms of the objects in the visible world. At this point, my illustration breaks down because, even if the person in the illustration could in theory go outside the house and see it from a larger perspective, we cannot go outside our world. Yet, just as the person in the illustration looked through windows and saw what were thought to be trees and birds, the facility of our minds called REASON senses that there are things beyond our world of time and space. Our apprehensions of goodness and beauty, our longings inspired by music, or our encounter with the sublime in nature, speak to us of a world beyond the visible and observable world, and it is this part of our experience that is met and satisfied by religion. Coleridge was very clear that great mischief could be done if the attempt was made to explain by the UNDERSTANDING, things that properly belonged to the sphere of REASON.

Let us go back, for a moment, to lice. No doubt it might be possible, scientifically, to explain the place of lice in the chain of being in the universe. However, to think that that would then prove the existence of God is to confuse UNDERSTANDING and REASON in Coleridge's sense. It would be to use an empirical explanation to describe a spiritual conviction. The same is true of the 'All things bright and beautiful' approach. What it attempts is a logical demonstration of God's existence, when the real purpose of beauty in nature is to touch and move us personally.

In two essays by Arthur Clutton-Brock there is criticism of the view that science alone can explain the whole of reality as we experience it.[37] He points out the importance of music, and that in music, art escapes from all facts that can be seen or stated in words or paint, while at the same time music can touch and move us personally. He goes on to say that when we perceive beauty in nature and art, what we perceive are not objects but what he calls universal relations. The most important thing about beauty is that it is not *useful*. To see objects as beautiful is to see them in a new way: not as objects, but as indicators of something else that can be of no direct use to us but which can make us aware of a realm of values which we do not wish to master, but which we desire in some way to embrace. This in turn changes our relation to nature. Technical reason sees nature as an object to be used for the benefit of the human race, and this is not wrong in principle. But REASON as defined by Coleridge would see nature as a realm of spiritual experience in which we encounter awe, wonder and beauty. This approach is fully in accord with the Bible. In Psalm 8 we read the following words:

---

[37] A. Clutton-Brock, 'Spiritual Experience' and 'Spirit and Matter' in B. H. Streeter (ed.), *The Spirit. God and his relation to man considered from the standpoint of Philosophy, Psychology and Art*, London: Macmillan 1919, pp. 279-309, 312-346.

For I will consider thy heavens, even the works of thy fingers:
the moon and the stars which thou hast ordained.
What is man that thou art mindful of him:
And the son of man, that thou visitest him?

The psalmist sees the heavens and the moon and the stars not merely as objects. They arouse in him an experience of awe and wonder. These experiences are not useful to him in any practical way. They point beyond the objects themselves to a dimension that is beyond his comprehension.

I want at this point to quote an important passage from William Temple's book 'Christus Veritas'. Speaking of the articles of the Christian creed he writes that 'All the articles of the creed name objects of practical trust. When a man says "I believe in God" he ought not to mean that after a careful review of the evidence he inclines to the opinion that there probably exists a Being who may not improperly be called God; he ought to mean "I put my trust in God; I am determined to live in reliance on his love and power'.[38] To conclude that there probably exists a being who may not improperly be called God is to make a judgement from the realm of the UNDERSTANDING as defined by Coleridge. To say 'I put my trust in God; I am determined to live in reliance on his love and power' is to make a commitment based on the use of REASON as defined by Coleridge.

If this is correct, if the path to the kind of believing commitment described by William Temple is via REASON and not

---

[38] W. Temple, *Christus Veritas. An Essay*, London: Macmillan & Co., 1924, p. 266.

UNDERSTANDING, how does this believing commitment come about? The answer is that it comes as a response to proclamation or preaching. Paul is our best guide here. In his First letter to the Corinthians we read,

> For after that in the wisdom of God the world by wisdom knew not God, it pleased God by the foolishness of preaching to save them that believe. For the Jews require a sign, and the Greeks seek after wisdom: but we preach Christ crucified, unto the Jews a stumbling block, and unto the Greeks foolishness; but unto them which are called, both Jews and Greeks, Christ the power of God, and the wisdom of God. (1 Corinthians 1.21-23)

Proclamation or preaching can take various forms. It can be done via a liturgical service, and it is Paul who reminds us that when we celebrate the Lord's Supper 'as often as ye eat this bread, and drink this cup, ye do shew the Lord's death till he come' (1 Corinthians 11.26), where the Greek verb translated 'shew' in the Authorised Version is *katangelein*, meaning 'to proclaim', which is how the Revised Standard Version renders it. Proclamation can also come via hymns, and in the English-speaking tradition one thinks especially of the hymns of Isaac Watts and Charles Wesley. Proclamation can be done by a way of dramatic enactment of the events of Holy Week and Good Friday, as well as by preaching in the context of a service. What happens in preaching and proclamation, in whatever form, is that we give expression to an initiative towards us that has come from God. As Paul puts it, 'we preach not ourselves, but Christ Jesus the Lord; and ourselves your servants for Jesus' sake. For God, who commanded the light to shine out of darkness, hath shined in our hearts, to give the light of the knowledge of the glory of God in the face of Jesus Christ'. (2 Corinthians 4.5-6).

The fact that the initiative in proclamation comes from God accounts for the apparent absurdity of the message. If it had been left to human understanding to devise a religion, would it have devised something that required us to look at a crucified criminal and to say 'This is the Son of God, the Saviour of the world?' It is, perhaps, at this point that we can see most clearly the distinction between the role of UNDERSTANDING and the role of REASON, as defined by Coleridge, in regard to the Christian faith. The attempt to prove the existence of God by looking at 'all things bright and beautiful' is totally different from pointing to a man on the cross and inviting people to put their trust in the God who is there revealed.

In his 'Aids to Reflection', Coleridge called attention to the mischief that can be caused when UNDERSTANDING and REASON are not properly distinguished, and when UNDERSTANDING is applied to things that are beyond the sphere of empirical experience. In the final part of this lecture, I want to explore this in relation to Christian belief today, using as my example, the so-called Apostles' Creed. Now I would not claim that this creed is an adequate statement of Christian belief. It says nothing about the Bible, the church, the sacraments, or the atonement. Yet I am happy to recite it in church services, thereby identifying myself with the Christian tradition that wrote it and has preserved it.

If the proper distinction between REASON and UNDERSTANDING is not made, two errors can arise. On the one hand, it can be maintained that in order to be a Christian, a person must believe wholeheartedly in every clause of the creed. On the other hand, because some of these clauses are problematic, the conclusion may be drawn that the creed is useless and that its presence in public worship is an embarrassment.

Around the beginning of 1906, a fellow of an Oxford College wrote to the Bishop of Oxford asking to be considered for ordination. As a fellow of an Oxford College he had the right to be considered for ordination, and he sent the Bishop a statement of his beliefs, including his view that he could only accept the doctrine of the Virgin Birth very tentatively. The previous year he had written to a friend that he was 'pretty clear' that the Virgin Birth ought not to be in the creed.[39] Because of this, the Bishop of Oxford decided that he could not accept the young man for ordination. Fortunately for the subsequent history of the Church of England, this young man had an advantage. His father had been the previous Archbishop of Canterbury, and on the strength of this he got himself invited to Lambeth Palace to discuss his situation with the then Archbishop of Canterbury. The upshot of all this was that he was ordained by the Archbishop of Canterbury in the December of 1908. If he had not had this advantage, the Church of England might have been deprived of its greatest Archbishop for 1,000 years, namely, Archbishop William

---

[39] See F. A. Iremonger, *William Temple. Archbishop of Canterbury. Life and Letters,* London: Oxford University Press, 1948, p. 106. See also pp. 108- 123 for the events leading to Temple's ordination.

Temple. Temple's difficulty was not unique then, nor since. In 1962 I spent the summer term at Saint George's College, Jerusalem, together with about 20 other ordinands. We were invited to tea by the wife of the Dean of the cathedral. She was very firm in her opinions, and she left us in no doubt, that unless we could believe all the articles of the creed, and especially the Virgin Birth, we ought not to be offering ourselves for ordination.

If you look at the Apostles' Creed, it will be clear that some of its causes have to do with UNDERSTANDING and that some have to do with REASON. For example, that Jesus suffered under Pontius Pilate, was crucified, dead and buried, are statements of facts of history, history that can be verified by documents other than those in the New Testament. However, where does the Virgin Birth fit in? Is it a matter of UNDERSTANDING, or a matter of REASON? The historical evidence for the Virgin Birth is uncertain. The Gospels of Matthew and Luke state that Jesus was born of a virgin. However, the Virgin Birth is not mentioned anywhere else in the New Testament, it forms no part of the apostolic preaching, and there are hints in the Gospels that suggest that Jesus had two natural parents. At Mark 6.3, one of the earliest papyrus witnesses to the text has 'is this not the carpenter's son?', a reading that was soon corrected to 'is this not the carpenter?' in order to remove the suggestion that Jesus really was Joseph's son.[40] Oliver Quick, in his book 'Doctrines of the Creed', is quite clear that the historical

---

[40] See V. Taylor, *The Text of the New Testament. A Short Introduction*, London: Macmillan & Co., 1961, pp. 83-4.

evidence is inconclusive.[41]   He goes on to say that it is theology that must determine our belief whether or not the Virgin Birth is a historical fact. This is a classic example of the confusion between REASON and UNDERSTANDING, from a theologian whom I greatly admire and respect. Theology can never decide matters of history. Only historical evidence can do that. However, Quick is fair-minded enough to allow that there will be people who "may prefer to think that, inasmuch as the manhood of Jesus was no superhumanity but our own human nature spiritually fashioned anew by an amazing act of divine condescension, the physical conditions of its conception and birth did not vary from those which nature ordinarily requires".[42]   This was not Quick's own view, but he was suffi-ciently sensitive to the issues involved to see that any dogmatic insistence that an ordinand must 'believe in' the Vir-gin Birth in order to be ordained was unacceptable. And we must add, that such insistence would not only confuse REASON and UNDERSTANDING, but would fail to see the distinction be-tween 'believing in' and 'believing that'.

There are, however, clauses in the Apostles' Creed that clearly belong to the sphere of REASON, not UNDERSTANDING. Principal among them would be the first clause, 'I believe in God, the Father Almighty, Maker of heaven and earth', and the second clause, 'and in Jesus Christ his only Son our Lord'. As I hope that this lecture will have made clear, belief in God as creator is not a deduction from the visible universe, but a response of

---

[41] O. C. Quick, *Doctrines of the Creed. Their Basis in Scripture and their Meaning Today*, London: Nisbet & Co., 1938, p. 158.
[42] Quick, *Doctrines*, p. 161

faith to the proclamation of the Gospel. The same is true of the second clause; but in the history of theology, many attempts have been made, by using UNDERSTANDING, to 'demonstrate' the sonship of Jesus. One method has been to take one of the 'I am' sayings from St. John's Gospel and to say on the basis of it, that Jesus was either insane, or a liar, or telling the truth, with the emphasis on the third possibility. Or attention has been drawn to the account of the miracles of Jesus in the Gospels as proof of his divinity, ignoring the fact that Jesus said that it was an evil generation that looked for such signs (Matthew 12.39). A third approach has been that of the fulfilment of Old Testament prophecies in the life and ministry of Jesus. What all these approaches overlook is that the divinity of Jesus consists of the fact that he is able to help us to come to trusting and loving faith in God, wherever his words and works are proclaimed and that this 'coming to faith' belongs to the sphere of REASON, not UNDERSTANDING.

An opposite application of UNDERSTANDING to the second clause of the creed can question whether it is, in fact, true. We are back where we were last week, with the point that it is possible to interpret the Gospels in ways that produce a Jesus quite different from the Jesus of the church's belief. Also, throughout the history of the church there have been attacks on the divinity of Jesus on various grounds: for example, that God is essentially Spirit, and cannot be manifested in human flesh. A popular form of the objection is that Jesus might have been a great moral or religious teacher, but he cannot have been the Son of God. The implication here is that we already know what God is like, and on the basis of this, we conclude that

Jesus cannot have been divine while at the same time being fully human. The Christian affirmation is that 'God was in Christ' (2 Corinthians 5.19) and that by responding to the message of what God has done in Jesus Christ we are drawn to faith in God.

English philosophy, as opposed to German philosophy (this is a dangerous generalisation, of course), has always tended to be one-dimensional; to prefer either/or to both/and. German philosophy is much more ready to be dialectical, to accept that reality, from a human perspective, is sufficiently messy and ambiguous to deny to human understanding the possibility that reality can be described in straightforward terms. Dialectical thinking accepts that it may be necessary to try to explain reality in terms of contradictions – by holding together contradictory statements. Luther's theology was dialectical, as in declarations such as that we are simultaneously sinners and justified by God's grace. We owe to Coleridge the fact that he was able to break free of the one-dimensional thinking in mechanistic and deterministic terms with which he had grown up, and to formulate the distinction between REASON and UNDERSTANDING with which this lecture has been concerned. I hope that I have done a little to demonstrate its importance for Christian belief and proclamation today, as part of what we owe to the 'broad church' of the nineteenth century.

LECTURE 4

Broad Church: Tradition

In the hymn by John Henry Newman 'Firmly I believe and truly', the following verse occurs,

> And I hold in veneration,
> For the love of him alone,
> Holy church as his creation,
> And her teachings as his own.

We used to have great fun with this verse at theological college, and used to tease the Anglo-Catholics by asking them whether they believed this, and if so, whether they accepted the infallibility of the Pope, and the Immaculate Conception and Assumption of the Blessed Virgin Mary. However, the verse expresses a problem for the Church of England just as much as for the Church of Rome. You will remember that last week I described how Bishop Paget of Oxford declined to accept William Temple for ordination because Temple could only very tentatively accept the Virgin Birth. What worried Paget was that he might ordain someone who would be authorised to teach, in the name of the church, a doctrine of which he was not completely sure.[43] I often used to hear the same argument when I was training for ordination. The argument went that an ordained priest should teach the faith of the church, and keep any private reservations to himself. I found that view intolerable then, and I find it intolerable today.

Underlying this argument was the following view of tradition. Jesus entrusted the Christian faith to the first disciples, they passed it on to their successors, and they passed it on to further successors, so that the teaching of the church today is guaranteed by this succession of teaching. A further point is that this is also guaranteed by the so-called apostolic succession of bishops, whose historic task it is to teach and preserve the faith.

There is an element of truth in this. In the first two centuries of the existence of the church, the gospel was threatened from several types of false teaching. One of them denied that Jesus had been truly human, while another denied that he had been truly God. In addition, there were groups represented by the so-called Gospel of Thomas and the so-called Gospel of Mary which claimed to preserve secret teachings of Jesus which he had given to followers such as Thomas or Mary Magdalene. There is no doubt that the idea of a chain of teachers transmit-

---

[43] F. A. Iremonger, *William Temple, Archbishop of Canterbury*, p. 109.

ting the authentic gospel helped to preserve the early church from being corrupted or subverted by these teachings. On the other hand, it was not quite as straightforward as this. It is clear from the letters of Paul to the Galatians and the Corinthians that there were people in the Jerusalem church who disputed Paul's right to preach the gospel and who claimed that his version of Christianity was false. We can only be grateful that Paul and the churches founded by him were able to resist these accusations, as well as the erroneous teachings about Jesus that abounded in the days of the early church. However, the fact that some form of tradition in the early church saved it from corruption by false teachings should not commit us to the view of tradition that is implied in the verse from the hymn that I quoted just now. Tradition is not an adding on process by which you simply add on to what you already have. Tradition, in the Christian sense, must be a continual critical engagement with what has been passed down, in the light of new knowledge and new thinking. It was critical engagement with tradition that led Saint Norbert to found the order of Canons that ministered here in the Abbey for 350 years, and it was critical engagement which made Martin Luther challenge the church of his day, and bring about the Reformation. In this evening's lecture I shall try to describe some of the ways in which a broad church today can understand and use tradition.

I shall begin by speaking of the importance of studying the **history of tradition**. For many years I taught a course in Sheffield entitled 'The use of the Bible in social and moral questions'. I approached the subject historically, by showing how the Bible had been used in previous centuries and in different Christian traditions. For example, on the matter of the divorce and remarriage of people, something which the Church of England has only very recently, and grudgingly come to accept, I was able to point out that for the great reformers, Luther and Calvin, whose commitment to the Bible could not be questioned, divorce and remarriage was certainly allowable in some cases.[44] This was also the view of the great Puritan scholar Richard Baxter. Another interesting topic was whether the Bible teaches that if Christians are going to eat meat, it should be kosher or halal meat. Not only is it clearly taught in Genesis 9.4 that meat should not be eaten with the blood, the law is restated in Leviticus 17.12, and in Acts 15 at the Council of Jerusalem it is decided that non-Jews who become Christians should observe that part of the mosaic law that prohibits the eating of blood (Acts 15.29). It could therefore be claimed, as some Christian writers have done in the past, that the prohibition against eating blood has the highest authority, being commanded by God to Noah, reaffirmed by Moses, and renewed by the apostles acting under the guidance and instruction of the Holy Spirit.[45] Yet I have never met any Christians today, including the strictest Bible-believing Christians, who were even aware of the matter, let alone prepared to take it seriously. I found that approaching things historically in this way enabled students to engage critically with tradition, in a way that did not immediately threaten their

---

[44] See my *According to the Scriptures? The Challenge of using the Bible in Social, Moral and Political Questions*, London: Equinox, 2007, pp. 87-95
[45] See my *An Introduction to the Bible*, Sheffield: Equinox, 2023 (3rd ed.), pp. 147-8.

own positions, but which led them to reconsider why it was that they accepted the views that they did.

Another way of engaging critically with tradition is to study the **history of Biblical interpretation**. When this is done, it becomes clear that the interpretation of the Bible has always been critical in the sense that interpreters have applied to the text their knowledge of science and of human growth and development, and the evidence of other passages in the Bible. As I mentioned in the discussion two weeks ago, the Hebrew text of 1 Samuel 13.1 states that Saul was one year old when he began to reign. The text is obviously corrupt, but this is what has been preserved as the canonical text. That Saul was aged one year when he began to reign is obviously impossible from the point of view of human growth and development, and also because in the following chapter Saul is said to have a son Jonathan who is a young man, which probably means that he was at least 14 years old. As far as I am aware, no attempt has ever been made to argue that the text must be accepted as true. Rather, various attempts have been made to get round the difficulty. Early Christian commentators, following Jewish scholars, said that it meant that Saul was as innocent as a child aged one year when he began his reign. Another ancient Jewish solution, followed by the Authorised Version of the Bible, was to mistranslate the Hebrew to mean that Saul reigned one year before he summoned all Israel to gather before him.

We also mentioned in discussion two weeks ago Augustine's great work the 'City of God' written early in the fifth century, in which Augustine dealt with a number of difficulties in the opening chapters of Genesis, such as why light is created on first day but the sun and moon are not created until the fourth day. What sort of light was it that God created on the first day? Again, were the long years lived by people in Genesis 5, running in some cases to over 900 years, the same length as years that we experience, or were they different? In the 12th century the great Jewish philosopher, Maimonides argued that all the prophecies and miracles in the Old Testament occurred in visions to those who were involved. He based this on Genesis 15.1 which says that God spoke to Abram in a vision, and for Maimonides, this statement controlled all other passages in the Old Testament that recorded prophecies and miracles. They all occurred in visions, not in the normal world of experience, and therefore they did not violate any scientific laws. I could give many other illustrations to show that it was not in the 19th century that people first began to have difficulties about miraculous and other stories in the Bible, but that this had been the case from the very earliest days of Biblical interpretation.[46] Knowing this does not, of course, necessarily help us to interpret the difficult passages, but it stops us from feeling guilty about reading the biblical text critically and honestly.

Last week I was speaking of William Temple's difficulties with the Virgin Birth. It is not widely known that in 1938 the Church of England published a report entitled 'Doctrine in the Church of England', the report of a commission that had been

---

[46] See my chapter 'An Outline of the History of Old Testament Study' in J. W. Rogerson (ed.), *Beginning Old Testament Study*, London: SPCK, 1998 (new edition), pp. 6-24.

chaired by Archbishop Temple, in which it was clearly stated and acknowledged that some members of the commission felt that the doctrine of the Virgin Birth diminished the humanity of Jesus, and impaired his complete identification with the human race.[47]   Although this was a minority view among members of the commission, the report made it clear that to be uncertain about the Virgin Birth did not mean that a person did not accept the full divinity of Christ. Indeed, it could be argued that denying the Virgin Birth made the claim that God was in Christ even more wonderful than if Jesus had had a miraculous birth. It was ignorance of this report that led to assertions that people should not be ordained if they could not accept the Virgin Birth.

What I have said so far may seem to have been negative, but I have not intended it to be so. We are told in John's Gospel (John 8.32) that the truth will make us free, and I have known many students to be liberated by gaining an historical perspective on the history of biblical interpretation and its use in social and moral questions, and by discovering that if they had difficulties with some details of miracles, they were by no means the first to do so. It is tragic when Christians find themselves in churches where tradition is used and understood in such a way as to make members feel that they cannot be honest with themselves and that they must leave their brains and critical faculties behind at the church door when they enter the church building. It should be added that critical

---

[47] *Doctrine in the Church of England. The Report of the Commission on Christian Doctrine appointed by the Archbishops of Canterbury and York in 1922*, London: SPCK, 1938, pp. 81-3.

engagement with the history of tradition was characteristic of the broad churchmen of the 19th century. Coleridge, for example, looked back to the work of the Anglican so-called Cambridge Platonists of the 17th century[48] and also engaged with the writings of Bishop Jeremy Taylor and Archbishop Robert Leighton.

The next part of tradition that I want to discuss is that of **church hymns**. In the Lutheran tradition, of course, these play an enormous role, especially in the way that the tunes of the hymns were used by J.S. Bach in his preludes and cantatas. Not only Luther himself, but other great hymn writers adorn this tradition, including Paul Gerhard in the 17th century and Jochen Klepper in the 20th century, who took his own life together with those of his Jewish wife and younger daughter to save them from being taken to Nazi death camps. Some of the best German hymns have been translated into English, such as 'Now thank we all our God', 'Praise to the Lord the Almighty, the King of creation' and 'All my hope on God is founded', and it is not widely known that John Wesley translated a number of German hymns for use in his own work.

In the English-speaking tradition of hymn writing two great representatives are Isaac Watts and Charles Wesley, and their importance lies in their marvellous ability to state Christian belief profoundly in poetic language. Take for example, the final verse of Wesley's well-known hymn 'Love divine all loves excelling'. You will remember that it goes as follows:

---

[48] See B. Willey, *The English Moralists*, pp. 176, 183, 300, 305.

Finish then thy new creation,
Pure and spotless let us be;
Let us see thy great salvation,
Perfectly restored in thee.
Changed from glory into glory,
Till in heaven we take our place,
Till we cast our crowns before thee,
Lost in wonder, love, and praise.

Some of the language comes straight from the Bible. 'Changed from glory into glory' comes from 2 Corinthians 3.18 while 'casting crowns' comes from the great vision of the worship of heaven in Revelation 4.10. The idea of the new creation comes from 2 Corinthians 5.17, the passage that says that if anyone is in Christ he is a new creature or new creation. These images are then combined together in order to produce profound theology. The person who is grasped by and responds to divine love is a new creation, but this cannot be a completed work in this world. It can only be a work in progress and the task of making the believer pure and spotless is achieved as he or she gazes upon the face of Christ. But this is not a work in progress whose completion will benefit only the individual concerned. Its completion will sum up the great universal salvation accomplished in Christ. All these profound thoughts are in expressed eight lines of simple poetry.

In the well-known Christmas Carol 'Hark the herald angels sing', come the following lines:

Veiled in flesh the Godhead see!
Hail the incarnate deity!
Pleased as man with man to dwell,
Jesus our Emmanuel.

Four lines of poetry express the mystery of the Incarnation and the humanity and divinity of Christ!

A remarkable hymn by Charles Wesley which I have never heard sung in an Anglican church has the following first verse:

> Let earth and heaven combine,
> Angels and men agree,
> To praise in songs divine
> The incarnate deity,
> Our God contracted to a span,
> Incomprehensibly made man.

The second verse is just as remarkable.

> He laid his glory by,
> He wrapped him in our clay;
> Unmarked by human eye,
> The latent Godhead lay;
> Infant of days he here became,
> And bore the mild Immanuel's name.

Almost certainly the best known hymn of Isaac Watts is "When I survey the wondrous cross" which is a marvellous version of Paul's exclamation in Galatians 6.14 "but God forbid that I should glory, save in the cross of our Lord Jesus Christ, by whom the world is crucified unto me, and I unto the world." Other well-known hymns by Watts include "Come, let us join our cheerful songs with the angels round the throne" and "Jesus shall reign where'er the sun". The importance of hymns in enabling us not only to worship but also to form and inform the theology by which we live, cannot be overestimated, and the fact that schools no longer have formal acts of worship in which these hymns are used is not only a matter of great regret, but an actual and potent threat to the knowledge and practice of Christianity in this country. I grew up in a family that had little or no contact with the church or Christianity but I can still remember learning the hymn "Jesus shall reign" at primary school, and being thrilled by it.

I now want to say something about the importance of **sermons** as part of tradition. Several years before I retired from Sheffield University, I taught a course entitled the Use of the Bible in Preaching. As far as I am aware, this was unique in the British University system, and yet the use of the Bible in preaching must far exceed any other use when you consider the number of sermons preached every Sunday and that this has been going on for two thousand years in the universal church! Of course, only the best sermons get published, which is just as well! The broad church Anglicans of the 19th century are well represented here. In the first lecture I quoted from several of the remarkable sermons by F.W. Robertson of Brighton. I also have on my bookshelves many volumes of sermons by F.D. Maurice, and Charles Kingsley, similarly, published sets of sermons. Much can be learned from these, not only about the broad church movement, but about Christian theology, in a profound way. The 20th century also produced its great preachers and their published sermons. I was greatly helped in my early steps in Christian faith by the sermons of the Methodist preacher Leslie Weatherhead, and I was also able to hear him preach at the City Temple in London on several occasions. Two things impressed me deeply about Weatherhead's preaching. First of all, it was absolutely honest. If there were difficulties in the text or doctrine that he was expounding he faced and recognized them head on. This was most encouraging to someone like myself with an exceedingly critical and questioning mind, and surrounded by people who told me that I must teach 'what the church believed', whatever my own mental reservations might be. Secondly, Weatherhead made it clear to his listeners that he was a committed disciple of Jesus Christ and that his aim in preaching was to help others in their discipleship. This combination of honesty and positive preaching was an important part of my own formation.

This observation leads me to make what I think is the most important point in this evening's lecture. It is that tradition, however we understand it, should be liberating and not imprisoning. What I have called the add-on theory of tradition, something that has to be maintained by the church at all costs, and which has to be accepted by Christians whether they can do so honestly or not, is definitely not liberating. Critical engagement with the past, with the way that the Bible has been used, or with the history of theology, is liberating. It sees tradition not in terms of believing about, or believing that, but in terms of believing *in* the God who in Jesus Christ brings hope and life. In other words, tradition must be a means to an end, the end being living faith in God, and not an end in itself. Other great preachers of the 20th century who could be mentioned here include the Lutheran preacher Helmut Thielicke, who was a member of the Confessing Church in Germany, the church that actively opposed Hitler, and who preached to large crowds in Hamburg in the closing days of the war and in the difficult days of the post-war period in

Germany. His sermons on the parables of Jesus translated into English under the title "The Waiting Father" are full of great insights.[49] Another German Lutheran, who had to take refuge in the United States, and who preached remarkable sermons was Paul Tillich. Two fine collections go under the arresting titles "The Shaking of the Foundations" and "The Eternal Now".[50]

The last aspect of tradition that I want to talk about in this evening's lecture is **collections of prayers**. It is arguable that I ought also to talk about worship as part of tradition, but that would make this lecture too long, and I shall say something about worship in the final lecture next week. Like collections of sermons at their best, collected prayers at their best contain the accumulated wisdom and experience of people's encounter with God over many generations. Although they can be no substitute for our own prayers they can deepen our faith and help us to feel that we are part of a great tradition stretching back over centuries, of people who have trusted in God and were not disappointed. Many years ago I bought at a church jumble sale an original 1936 edition of the BBC prayer book used in connection with the daily service and entitled "New every morning". I still use this almost every day as the basis for my own prayers. One of my favourites from this collection is one that we used when the Abbey was recently rededicated by the Archbishop of York. It goes as follows:

---

[49] H. Thielicke, *The Waiting Father. Sermons on the parables of Jesus,* London: James Clarke & Co, 1960
[50] P. Tillich, *The Eternal Now. Sermons,* London: SCM Press, 1963

> Oh God of unchangeable power and eternal light, look
> favourably on thy whole church, that wonderful and sacred
> mystery; and, by the tranquil operation of thy perpetual
> providence, carry out the work of man's salvation. And let the
> whole world feel and see that things which were cast down
> are being raised up, that those which had grown old are being
> made new, and that all things are returning to perfection
> through him from whom they took their origin; even through
> our Lord Jesus Christ.

Lastly, it may be objected that, in this lecture, I have failed to stress the significance of tradition in safeguarding the Christian faith from error and false teaching. This is a particularly important issue at the present time. The Church of England is deeply and bitterly divided. On the one hand there are those who feel that the catholic tradition of the Church of England is at risk. On the other hand, there are those who feel that, at all costs, they must maintain its reformed tradition. Alternative episcopal oversight has been provided for the first group within the organisation of the Church of England. The other group have set up their own institutional arrangements outside the Church of England but within the Anglican Communion.

A broad church view of this might be as follows. I allowed at the beginning of this lecture that it was important for the early church to maintain a succession of teaching in order to ensure the essential truth of the gospel. However, I am equally clear that the church owes much to people in its history who have been prepared to break with received tradition, and to go their own way. Where would the church be without Saint Francis, or Martin Luther, or George Fox the founder of the Quakers, or John Wesley? And we must not forget that F.D. Maurice himself was dismissed from his post at King's College, London, in 1853 because of his alleged false theology. The man responsible for his dismissal was Dr. Jelf. Today, Maurice is widely and deeply studied as one of the greatest Anglican thinkers of the 19th century. If Jelf is remembered at all today, it is only as the person who was responsible for Maurice's dismissal!

It seems to me that we must do two things. First, we must believe and trust in the Holy Spirit. We must believe and trust that if we do our work honestly and prayerfully, God's Spirit will overrule what is bad in our work and will use what is good in the furtherance of his kingdom. Second, we must believe in the Gamaliel principle.

In Acts chapter 5, when the apostles are brought before the Jewish Council and reminded that they had been strictly charged not to preach about Jesus, a member of the council named Gamaliel warns his colleagues not to be too hasty. He reviews the recent history of his people and how several revolutionary movements have come to nothing. He concludes with the words,

> refrain from these men, and let them alone: for if this counsel or this work be of men, it will come to naught: but if it to be of God, ye cannot overthrow it; less haply ye be found even to fight against God. (Acts 5.38-39).

As a lawyer might say, here I rest my case.

LECTURE 5

Broad Church Today

A broad church today is biblical, evangelical, and catholic, and in this final lecture I shall discuss each of these terms in the light of what I have been saying in the previous lectures. I begin with **the Bible**. The Bible is an astonishing human achievement, yet it would not exist at all if God did not wish to communicate with the human race and enter into fellowship with it. The Bible exists because of God's initiative. People did not write it down because they wanted to further their own interests or to lord it over others. To me, one of the remarkable things about the Bible is the way that it shows that those who hear the call of God and respond to it become involved in a ministry of considerable suffering. Further, because it would be callous to suppose that God causes people to suffer in his name without suffering himself, we can see in the sufferings of his servants what it costs God to be involved in our world in such a personal way.

I shall now illustrate this from the way in which a number of great people are portrayed in the Old Testament. As I said in a previous lecture, these are not historical narratives in the modern sense, but the product of the cultural memory of the people of God. The personages are therefore representatives of the experiences of many people who were in different ways involved with the call of God.

Abraham, the founder of the nation, is asked to leave his home and to migrate to a far-off land about which he knows nothing, and where he experiences famine almost as soon as he has arrived (Genesis 12.1-3, 10). He suffers the agony of believing that God wishes him to offer his only son in sacrifice (Genesis 22). Although this is not required, this does not lessen the pain and anguish of Abraham as he makes the journey to the appointed place and faces the possibility of having to commit an appalling act.

Moses, the great leader of his people at the time of the Exodus, has to endure the constant complaint and criticism of the people he has led to freedom, and because of the obstinacy of the people, he is condemned, with them, not to enter the promised land but to view it only from a distance. David, the greatest of the kings of the Old Testament, is presented as a flawed character, one who becomes guilty of adultery and murder, and who pays the penalty for this by seeing his family disintegrate into fratricide, rape, and rivalry. Solomon, the great builder of Jerusalem and the temple, is shown to preside over a kingdom whose social divisions and injustices lead to its disintegration after his death.

The fate of some of the prophets resembles that of Moses. To Jeremiah is given the awful commission to preach that God is fighting against Jerusalem and will destroy it because of the sinfulness of the nation. His message brings threats against his life, imprisonment and, at the end of his life, exile in a place to which he does not wish to go, and where the people taunt him by saying that their troubles have come about only because they took notice of his preaching (Jeremiah 44.15-19). In chapters 40 to 55 of the book of Isaiah there is portrayed a servant of God who during his lifetime is despised and rejected (Isaiah 53.3).

It comes as no surprise that in the New Testament the ministry of Jesus is ultimately one of suffering and apparent failure. Even his closest disciples do not understand the nature of his mission, and at the time when he faces mocking, torture, and the unimaginable pain of crucifixion, his closest male followers desert him, and deny that they ever knew him.

There is a remarkable passage in Isaiah 63 that states that 'in all their afflictions he [God] was afflicted' (Isaiah 63.9). The Bible is the record of what it costs individuals to respond to the call of God, and what it must therefore cost God himself. We can get some small idea of this by imagining how parents suffer when they see their children undergoing suffering. That is what we might call the story-line of the Bible; but the Bible is also a library, including philosophical works such as Job and Ecclesiastes, which meditate profoundly upon the problem of innocent suffering, or there is that great treasury of psalms that range from awesome praise of God to anguished cries for help in the face of persecution, injustice, or physical illness, and the approach of death.

The Bible is essential for a broad church, but it must be the Bible read with the help of biblical criticism and with the benefit of the profound discussions that have taken place in the twentieth century about hermeneutics, or the theory of interpretation. It is at this point that a modern broad church is at its furthest distance from the great figures of the mid-19th century who otherwise are the source of so much inspiration. When F. D. Maurice, Charles Kingsley, and F. W. Robertson were active in their ministries, biblical criticism in Britain hardly existed and was regarded with the greatest suspicion. It was not until late in the 19th century that the churches in Britain were able to begin to come to terms with it. As late as 1881, the brilliant young Scottish scholar William Robertson Smith was dismissed from his post at the Free Church College in Aberdeen because of an article on the Bible that he had published in the ninth edition of the Encyclopaedia Britannica. We cannot blame Maurice, Kingsley and Robertson for being men of their time, but I am certain that if they were alive today, they would see the necessity of biblical criticism for presenting the Christian faith to intelligent, honest, and thoughtful people. What this means, is that a broad church must find ways of ensuring that its members are familiar with biblical criticism and modern methods of interpretation at their best, and have the confidence to see that they can liberate them from narrow views of biblical literalism. Much of my own popular writing over the past 40 years has been directed precisely to this end, but it is still, alas, the case that for the majority of people who attend church the Bible is an unread book and biblical criticism is seen as a threat to Christian belief. A broad church must emphasise the centrality of the Bible, must ensure that its members have an extensive knowledge of its content and that they know how biblical criticism and modern approaches to interpretation can throw great light on that content and help readers and listeners to encounter the God who speaks his word through its pages.

A broad church must be **evangelical** because it is biblical. If the Bible exists because of God's initiative in stretching out to the human race in love and mercy, the evangelistic task of a broad church must be to enable people to respond to that initiative. It is common ground among many churches that there is a gulf between God and humanity that has been caused by humanity's wickedness and evil. A broad church must take this seriously. The question is, how is that gulf bridged?

According to one view, God is so alienated by human wickedness that he cannot have fellowship with human beings unless the penalty for human wrongdoing is first paid by the sacrificial death of Christ. This view is not acceptable to a broad church because it is not in accord with the teaching of the Bible. Paul tells us that in Christ, God was reconciling the world to himself, not reconciling himself to the world (2 Corinthians 5.19). Further, the view that God cannot forgive sin until Christ has died on the cross makes nonsense of many passages in the Old Testament. When the Psalmist says in Psalm 103 'look how wide also the east is from the west: so far hath he set our sins from us' (Psalm 103.12), are we to suppose that the Psalmist does not mean what he says? Are we to suppose that he is not expressing his own joy at the experience of God's forgiveness, but is actually looking ahead to something that will only be possible in several hundred years' time, after Christ has died on the cross? When the psalmist prays in Psalm 51 'turn thy face from my sins: and put out all my misdeeds. Make me a clean heart, O God, and renew a right spirit within me' (Psalm 51.9-10), are we to suppose that this is a completely useless and pointless prayer, one which God cannot answer, because Christ will not die on the cross for many hundreds of years? In Romans 10.21 Paul quotes from Isaiah 65.2, 'all day long I have stretched forth my hands unto a disobedient and gainsaying people'. However, Paul and the writer of the Isaiah passage must have been mistaken. How could God stretch out his hands to a disobedient and gainsaying people if he was so repelled by their wickedness that he needed the sacrifice of Christ to enable him to draw near to them? In the previous verse, Paul also quotes from Isaiah 65.1 'I was found of them that sought me not; I was made manifest unto them that asked not after me'. However, again, this would be impossible on the view that without the sacrifice of Christ there can be no contact between God and sinful humanity. A further implication of this approach is that unless and until a person has accepted that Christ died for his sins, he must for ever remain alienated from God. A broad church will find quite unacceptable a use of the Bible which ignores its obvious meaning, and prefers instead a theory that makes nonsense of so much of what the Bible says.

A broad church approach sees the Old Testament as the record of God reaching out in love and mercy to a rebellious and disobedient people. Sometimes that love and mercy are recognized and accepted; sometimes not. God remains in touch with his people as much through his judgement as through his promises of salvation. In the New Testament God in Christ enters personally into the human wickedness which creates the gulf between the divine and human. He overcomes it by means of his selfless love on behalf of others, and he offers to God a perfect sacrifice of a life that has defeated sin and wickedness on behalf of others. In that he has represented the whole human race, the gap between God and humanity has been bridged. However, it is imperative for humans to know that this is the case. If someone deposits in my bank account a large sum of money, this is no use to me if I do not know about it or if I do not attempt to draw upon it. The evangelistic message of a broad church to individuals is that Christ has redeemed them, that they are sons and daughters of God not only by birth, but by adoption. God wishes them to know this in such a way that their lives are transformed, and that they are enabled to live in reliance and trust upon his mercy. The matter is put in this way in John's Gospel: 'this is life eternal, that they might know thee the only true God, and Jesus Christ, whom thou hast sent' (John 17. 3).

There is, however, one thing to be said for the view that God can only forgive sin because of Christ's sacrificial death. It makes it clear that forgiveness is always costly and can never overlook the nature of evil or regard it as other than it is. It emphasises that the justice of God must be satisfied. How does a broad church view take account of this? From a broad church perspective judgement is part of the good news. The Psalms look forward to the coming judgement of God. In Psalm 96 we have the following words

> let the heavens rejoice, and let the earth be glad: let the sea make a noise, and all that therein is. Let the field be joyful, and all that is in it: then shall all the trees of the wood rejoice before the LORD. For he cometh, for he cometh to judge the earth: and with righteousness to judge the world, and the people with his truth.

This is surely something we can all affirm. Surely we desire to live in a much better world than what human wickedness has made it. If God's judgement will deal with the wickedness in the world as well as that in our own lives, surely this is something to be welcomed. Judgement is part of the good news, because it is God's judgment, the God who in Jesus Christ enters into the world to bridge the gulf made by our wickedness. How that judgement will operate beyond the world of time we do not know, and should not presume to say, except to affirm, with F. D. Maurice, that judgement is not everlasting torture. We must have the courage and trust to believe that God will have the last word and in his own way will defeat and transform human wickedness.

I come, lastly, to the broad church as being **catholic**. By catholic I do not mean that the Church of England has bishops in the succession of the historic episcopate. I mean that it is catholic by being aware of its membership of the Church of Christ throughout the world. The Abbey, as a broad church, is part of the Church of England and the Anglican Communion, but it is more than that, and for this reason can and must take account of what is going on in churches beyond the Anglican communion including, in some cases, the Roman Catholic Church. A broad church must take account of what is happening in base communities in the Catholic Churches of Latin America, for example, and must be aware of the Liberation Theology that it has inspired and which is not, alas, part of the church scene in Britain. Also, it must accept that there are churches which do not have the historic episcopate but which theologically have much to teach us. Here, I think especially of the German Lutheran churches. This situation in some ways resembles that of the 19th century broad churchmen, while there are obviously great differences. In my first lecture I noted the importance of Germany and Lutheran theology for figures such as Coleridge, and for Julius Hare who was the mentor of Maurice and Kingsley. On the other hand, the 19th century broad churchmen could have had no conception of how the ecumenical movement of the 20th century and the German Church struggle of the 1930s would change how we must regard the church today. It is in the light of these developments that I shall now speak about the role of a broad church in the life of the nation, and my thinking here has been much shaped by several articles written in 1933 by Dietrich Bonhoeffer in response to the assumption of power in Germany in 1933 by Hitler's National Socialists.[51]

---

[51] D. Bonhoeffer, 'Der Führer und der Einzele in der jungen Generation' 'Dein Reich komme! Das Gebet der Gemeinde um Gottes Reich auf Erden'; 'Die Kirche vor der Judenfrage; Der Arier-Paragraph in der Kirche' in C. Gremmels, W. Huber (eds.), *Dietrich Bonhoeffer Auswahl. Band 2. Gegenwart und Zukunft der Kirche 1933-1935*, Gütersloh: Gütersloher Verlagshaus, 2006, pp. 47-88.

For Coleridge and Maurice the Church of England by law established was the national church and therefore had a role to play in the life of the nation. A modern broad church cannot accept this view. If we have learned anything from the German church struggle of the 1930s, it is that the church does not have its authority from the state but from God. The state also is an order ordained by God and must be seen in that light. One of the troubles with the traditional Anglican view of the relation between church and state is that it has seen these two institutions rather like two self-contained circles with the smaller circle representing the church embedded within a larger circle representing the state. We need, in fact, a model that shows the two institutions to be mutually dependent. We might think here in terms of a marriage. A husband cannot be a husband unless he has a wife, and vice versa. From a Christian perspective, the state cannot exist without the church and vice versa. At some periods in the history of the church, of course, the relationship has become one sided. In the Middle Ages the church had far too much power over the state and often controlled it. In today's world the state has far too much power over the Church, and tends to ignore it.

In May 1934 in the face of the threat to the church from the regime of Adolf Hitler, a Synod meeting in Barmen formulated the Barmen Declaration which became the basis of the Confessing Church.

I quote some extracts from that Declaration:

Scripture tells us that, in the as yet unredeemed world in which the Church exists, the State has by divine appointment the task of seeing to and maintaining - by the fullest exercise of human insight and human capacity, by means of the threat of force and by means of the use of force - law and peace. With gratitude and reverence towards God the Church acknowledges the benefit of this order which he has appointed. It is a reminder of God's kingdom, of God's commandment and righteousness, and so, of the responsibility of both rulers and ruled.

We reject the false doctrine that the State should or could go beyond its special task and become the sole and total order of human life, thus fulfilling also the Church's vocation.

We reject the false doctrine that the church should or could go beyond its special task and assume functions and dignities of the State, thus itself becoming an organ of the State.[52]

The important thing to notice about this quotation is that it is biblical. It claims that scripture tells us about the divine appointment and function of the state. This claim is best illustrated from the book of Deuteronomy where, in chapter 17, it is commanded that the King who sits on the throne of his kingdom must write out a copy of the divine law, that he should read it all the days of his life, that through it he may learn to fear the Lord his God, and that his heart shall not be lifted up above his brethren (Deuteronomy 17.18-20). In my opinion, the Church of England should assert as publicly as possible that as a part of the universal Church of Christ, even if it is a rather small part, it has a mandate from God to declare the true relationship between church and state. If its estab-

---

[52] A. Frey, *Cross and Swastika. The Ordeal of the German Church,* London: SCM Press, 1938, pp. 155-6.

lished position in England makes it difficult for the church to do this, it should be ready and willing to forgo its privileged position in law. In this way, it may save its life by losing it.

In his book entitled 'On the constitution of the Church and State', Coleridge stressed the importance of formulating an *idea* of the nation.[53] This derived from his distinction between REASON and UNDERSTANDING, which was the subject of the second lecture in this series, so that the idea was to be drawn from spiritual resources, especially the Bible, and human sensitivity and imagination. This is an important task for today's church, drawing upon all the theological resources of the worldwide church. For Coleridge, property was one of the pillars of his idea of the nation. In today's world, property has ceased to be a pillar and has become a major problem.[54] Property, in the sense of wealth, is responsible for the grotesque misdistribution of the world's resources not only between rich and poor nations but within rich and poor nations. The remarkable Jubilee legislation in Leviticus 25 decreed that every 50 years land was to revert to the original owners in order to prevent the type of accumulation of land and wealth which was so roundly condemned by the prophets of ancient Israel (Isaiah 5.8, 'Woe unto them that join house to house, that lay field to field, till there be no place'). If one of the tasks of the church is to proclaim the unity of the human

---

[53] S. T. Coleridge, *On the Constitution of the Church and State* (1830), London: J. M. Dent & Sons, 1972, pp. 3-23

[54] See especially U. Duchrow and F. J. Hinkelhammert, *Property for people, not for profit. Alternatives to the Global Tyranny of Capital,* London: Zed Books, 2004.

race in the sight of God, and that all humans are the children of God and therefore brothers and sisters to each other, it must wage an unceasing war against those systems that depend upon wealth and property to disfigure so disgracefully the relationships between human beings. The Kingdom of God is supposed to be a kingdom of right relationships. The human governance of the world without God has succeeded in establishing a kingdom of unrighteous relationships. Here, the battle is to be fought using the weapons of education, argument, and convincement. The Bible contains visions which must surely appeal to anyone with a modicum of sensitivity and a desire for fairness and justice. The church must concentrate on articulating this greater vision rather than fastening on particular issues, however important that they may be. If the church gives the impression that it is the Labour Party, or the Liberal Democratic Party, or even the Green Party at prayer, people will miss the larger vision which the church must articulate and proclaim, and will misunderstand what the church is and what its mission is.. The practical working out of the vision of a world that reflects God's lordship is not the business of the church, although that should not preclude the church from having practical agencies for helping the homeless, the destitute, and other casualties of the property-induced system.

In Coleridge's book on the constitution of the church and state, first published in 1830, Coleridge lamented the fact that education was becoming increasingly secularised.[55] For him,

---

[55] Coleridge, *Constitution*, p. 53.

this was a perversion of the proper distinction between REASON and UNDERSTANDING, and denoted the triumph of UNDER-STANDING, that is, empirical knowledge, over REASON, which was to do with aesthetic and spiritual knowledge. When we look at the education scene today, with the universities totally driven by matters of finance, it is hard to remember that universities developed from the cathedral schools of medieval Europe, and that the ancient universities were founded by the church. Again, the broad churchmen of the mid 19th century did much to promote education, especially for women, and for the working classes. A broad church today must see education as one of its top priorities, an education which should not be confined to but which should pay particular attention to the Bible, biblical criticism, and theology, precisely because these things hardly figure, if at all, in the state education system at all levels. The broad church should do this because of its mandate from God to proclaim and bring into effect its belief that without God humanity is incomplete. In the plans here at the Abbey which we are currently discussing we are hoping through publication and electronic means to do for our situation what the broad churchmen in the 19th century sought to do for theirs.

At the end of the first lecture I quoted from a sermon by F.W. Robertson of Brighton in which he saw the path that he was seeking to follow not as a middle way but as a deeper way. I hope that in these lectures I have given some indication of what a deeper way might mean for today's broad church.

The bibliography refers to books quoted in the footnotes. Readers who wish to read more about the main characters mentioned in the text are referred to the following works:

S. A. Brooke, *Life and Letters of Fred. W. Robertson, M. A.*, London: Kegan Paul, Trench, Trübner & Co, 1906

N. M. Distad, *Guessing at Truth. The Life of Julius Charles Hare*, Shepherdstown: The Patmos Press, 1979

R. Holmes, *Coleridge. Early Visions*, London: Hodder & Stoughton, 1989

R. Holmes, *Coleridge. Darker Reflections*, London: Harper Collins, 1998

F.Kingsley, *Charles Kingsley. His Letters and Memories of his life*, London: Macmillan & Co, 1890

F. Maurice, *The Life of Frederick Denison Maurice, chiefly told in his own letters*, 2 vols., London: Macmillan & Co., 1885

BIBLIOGRAPHY

C. K. Barrett, 'The Interpretation of the Old Testament in the New', in P. R. Ackroyd, C. F. Evans (eds.), *The Cambridge History of the Bible. From the Beginnings to Jerome*, Cambridge: Cambridge University Press, 1970, pp. 377-411

C. K. Barrett, *Jesus and the Gospel Tradition*, London: SPCK, 1967

D. Bonhoeffer, 'Der Führer und der Einzele in der jungen Generation' 'Dein Reich komme! Das Gebet der Gemeinde um Gottes Reich auf Erden'; 'Die Kirche vor der Judenfrage; Der Arier-Paragraph in der Kirche' in C. Gremmels, W. Huber (eds.), *Dietrich Bonhoeffer Auswahl. Band 2. Gegenwart und Zukunft der Kirche 1933-1935*, Gütersloh: Gütersloher Verlagshaus, 2006,

J. Calvin, *Genesis*, Edinburgh: Banner of Truth Trust, 1965 (original 1578)

A. Clutton-Brock, 'Spiritual Experience' and 'Spirit and Matter' in B. H. Streeter (ed.), *The Spirit. God and his relation to man considered from the standpoint of Philosophy, Psychology and Art*, London: Macmillan 1919, pp. 279-309, 312-346.

J. W. Colenso, *The Pentateuch and Book of Joshua Critically Examined*, London: Longman, Green, Longman, Roberts & Green, 1862

S. T. Coleridge, *Aids to Reflection in the Formation of a Manly Character on the Several Grounds of Prudence, Morality and Religion*, London: George Routledge & Sons (no date).

S. T. Coleridge, *On the Constitution of the Church and State* (1830), London: J. M. Dent & Sons, 1972

F. Copleston, *A History of Philosophy*, volume VI: Wolff to Kant, London: Burns and Oates, 1964

F. W. Cornish, *The English Church in the Nineteenth Century*, Part I, London: Macmillan & Co, 1910

Doctrine in the Church of England. The Report of the Commission on Christian Doctrine appointed by the Archbishops of Canterbury and York in 1922, London: SPCK, 1938

U. Duchrow and **F. J. Hinkelhammert**, *Property for people, not for profit. Alternatives to the Global Tyranny of Capital*, London: Zed Books, 2004

A. Frey, *Cross and Swastika. The Ordeal of the German Church*, London: SCM Press, 1938

J. C. Hare, *Charges to the Clergy of the Archdeaconry of Lewes*, Cambridge: (edited and with an Introduction by F. D. Maurice), Macmillan & Co, 1856

F. A. Iremonger, *William Temple. Archbishop of Canterbury. Life and Letters*, London: Oxford University Press, 1948

P. J. Jagger, *Clouded Witness. Initiation in the Church of England in The Mid-Victorian Period, 1850-1875*, Pennsylvania: Pickwick Publications, 1982

C. Kingsley, *The Gospel of the Pentateuch. A Set of Parish Sermons*, London: Parker, Son, and Bourn, 1863

F. D. Maurice, *The Patriarchs and Lawgivers of the Old Testament*, London: Macmillan & Co, 1892

N. Micklem, 'A Modern Approach to Christology' in G. K. A. Bell, A. Deissmann (eds.), *Mysterium Christi. Christological Studies by British and German Theologians*, London: Longmans, Green & Co., 1930

O. C. Quick, *Doctrines of the Creed. Their Basis in Scripture and their Meaning Today*, London: Nisbet & Co., 1938

C. E. Raven, *Christian Socialism 1848-1854*, London: Frank Cass & Co., 1968

F. W. Robertson, *Sermons Preached at Brighton*, Second Series, London: Kegan Paul, Trench,1889

J. W. Rogerson, *Old Testament Criticism in the Nineteenth Century: England and Germany*, London: SPCK, 1984

J. W. Rogerson, 'An Outline of the History of Old Testament Study' in J. W. Rogerson (ed.), *Beginning Old Testament Study*, London: SPCK, 1998 (new edition), pp. 6-24.

J. W. Rogerson, Judith M. Lieu, (eds.), *The Oxford Handbook of Biblical Studies*, Oxford: Oxford University Press, 2006

J. W. Rogerson, *According to the Scriptures? The Challenge of using the Bible in Social, Moral and Political Questions*, London: Equinox, 2007

J. W. Rogerson, *An Introduction to the Bible*, Sheffield: Equinox, 2013 (3rd ed.),

V. Taylor, *The Text of the New Testament. A Short Introduction*, London: Macmillan & Co., 1961

W. Temple, *Christus Veritas. An Essay*, London: Macmillan & Co., 1924

H. Thielicke, *The Waiting Father. Sermons on the parables of Jesus*, London: James Clarke & Co, 1960

P. Tillich, *The Eternal Now. Sermons*, London: SCM Press, 1963

E. R. Wickham, *Church and People in an Industrial City*, London: Lutterworth Press, 1957, pp.108-9.

B. Willey, *Nineteenth-Century Studies. Coleridge to Matthew Arnold*, Harmondsworth: Penguin Books, 1964

B. Willey, 'S. T. Coleridge (1772-1834)' in B. Willey, *The English Moralists*, London: Methuen, 1965, pp. 296-312

INDEX

Abraham 63
Ancient Israel, climate 34-5
Ancient Israel, history of 21-5
Apostles' Creed 41-44
Apostolic succession 48-9, 69
Argument from design for God's existence 32-4, 38
Atonement, the 14-15, 66-8
Augustine, *City of God* 52

Bach, J. S. 54
Baptism 5, 7-10
Barmen Declaration 71-2
Barrett, C. K. 27-30
Biblical criticism 21-2, 30, 65
Bonheoffer, D. 70
Bunsen, C. C. J. 6

Calvin, J. 23-4, 50
Cambridge Platonists 54
Chartism 14
Christ of faith, the 21, 27-9, 45
Church attendance in Sheffield 5-6
Church Census 1851 5
Church Census 1881 6
Christian Socialism 14
Church of England and Establishment 71

Clutton-Brock, A. 38-9
Colenso, J. W. 17-20, 30-1
Coleridge, S. T. 6, 12, 35-8, 40-1, 54, 71, 73, 74
Coplestone, F. 36
Cornish, F. W. 8
Cultural memory 24-5, 29

David, king of Israel 63
Dialectical thinking 46
Divorce and remarriage 50
Duchrow, U. 73

Education, state 74-5

Fox, G. 61
Frey, A. 72

Gamaliel principle 61
Gerhard, P. 54
Germany 3, 6, 11-12, 36, 46
German Church struggle, 1933-45 70
German Lutheranism 3-4, 70
Gorham, G. C. 7-8
Gorham controversy 7-8

Hare, J. C. 6, 11-12, 14, 20, 70
Hinkelhammert, F. J. 73
Hymns 54

Industrial revolution in
 Britain 5
Iremonger, F. A. 42, 48

Jagger, P. J. 7, 9
Jelf, R. W. 61
Jeremiah 64
Jesus 64
Jesus of history, the 21, 27-9,
 45
Jubilee legislation 73
Judgement, God's 69

Kant, I. 36
Kingsley, C. 6, 9-10, 13-14,
 20, 57, 65, 70
Klepper, J. 54

Leighton, R. 54
Liberation Theology 70
Ludlow, J. M. 14
Luther, M 46, 49, 5, 61
Lutheranism 3, 54

Maimonides, M. 52
Mary Magdalene 21
Maurice, F. D. 6, 9-10, 11-14,
 17-18, 20-21, 57, 61, 65, 6,
 70, 71
Meat, should Christians eat it
 with blood? 50-1
Micklem, N. 27
Moses 63

Newman, J. H. 47
Norbert of Xanten 49

Old Testament criticism
 21-2

Paul 40, 67
'Politics for the People' 14
Preaching 40-1

Quick, O. C. 43-4

Paget, F. 48
Property 73
Raven, C. E. 14
REASON, Coleridge's view of
 35-7, 40
Robertson, F. W. 6, 8-10, 14-
 15, 20, 57, 65, 7, 75
Rogerson, J. W. 6, 11, 18, 22,
 28, 50, 52

Scott, A. J. 14
Smith, W. R. 65
Solomon, king of Israel 63

Taylor, J. 54
Taylor, V. 43
Temple, W. 39-40, 42, 48, 53
Thielicke, H. 59
Tillich, P. 59
Tradition, history of 50-1

UNDERSTANDING, Coleridge's
 view of 35-7, 40
Virgin birth 42-4, 48, 53

Watts, I. 40, 55-7
Weatherhead, L. D. 58
Wesley, C. 40, 55-7
Wesley, J. 54, 61
Wickham, E. R. 5-6
Willey, B. 6, 36, 54

ABOUT THE AUTHOR

John William Rogerson was born in London in 1935 and educated at Bec School, Tooting, the Joint Services School for Linguists, Coulsdon Common, where he completed an intensive course in Russian, and the Universities of Manchester, Oxford and Jerusalem, where he studied theology and Semitic languages. He was ordained in 1964 and served as Assistant Curate at St. Oswald's, Durham. From 1964 to 1975 he was Lecturer, and from 1975 to 1979 Senior Lecturer in Theology at Durham University before moving in 1979 to become Professor and Head of the Department of Biblical Studies at the University of Sheffield, retiring in 1996. He was made an honorary Canon of Sheffield Cathedral in 1982 and an Emeritus Canon in 1995. In addition to many essays and scholarly articles, his published books include *Myth in Old Testament Interpretation* (1974), *Psalms* (Cambridge Bible Commentary, with J. W. McKay, 1977), *Anthropology and the Old Testament* (1978), *Old Testament Criticism in the Nineteenth Century: England and Germany* (1984), *The New Atlas of the Bible* (1985, translated into nine languages), *W. M. L. de Wette. Founder of Modern Biblical Criticism. An Intellectual Biography* (1991), *The Bible and Criticism in Victorian Britain. Profiles of F. D. Maurice and William Robertson Smith* (1995), *An Introduction to the Bible* (1999, 3rd edition 2012), *Theory and Practice in Old Testament Ethics* (2004), *According to the Scriptures? The Challenge of using the Bible in Social, Moral and Political Questions* (2007), *A Theology of the Old Testament. Cultural memory, communication and being human* (2009), *The Art of Biblical Prayer* (2011). He was awarded the degree of Doctor of Divinity for published work by the University of Manchester in 1975, and has also been awarded the Honorary Degree of Doctor of Divinity by the University of Aberdeen and the Honorary Degree of Dr. theol. by the Friedrich-Schiller-Universität, Jena and the Albert-Ludwigs-Universität, Freiburg im Breisgau.